My Four-Year Journey with our Risen Savior

Steven Kenneth Nelson's Testimony of Jesus Christ

Written by Steven Kenneth Nelson

Disclaimer

The following body of work has been written as non-fiction. The events which have been portrayed by the author are expressed with the best of his knowledge and recollection. All in all, it is a peek into the author's life and the emotions associated, so there is bound to be subjectivity. It is the truth comprehended by the author and not some fiction that is made up for writing this book.

Contents

Introduction

Greetings, my name is Steven Kenneth Nelson. Born November 29th, 1976. I have always just considered myself just a regular-type-fun-loving-God-loving American who just wants to get along with everybody. I come from a middle-class upbringing and, thankfully, I was raised a Christian. This testimony of Jesus Christ will focus primarily on the last 4 years from January 2020 through December 2023.

This book will go into detail about my divine encounters with our God. I want to be clear about something. I do not regard myself as more valuable than any other human soul. I am not claiming to be a Prophet. To tell you the truth, I have heard the term Prophet used in so many different contexts, that I don't think anybody knows exactly what it means anymore. I have heard it used for Pastors, people with Prophetic visions, people who are spreading the Gospel, and then there are the Prophets in Biblical names such as Moses and Isaiah. The list goes on and on. No, I am just going to tell my true-life story of my encounters with Christ and leave the labels for God to give.

I want to say something to the readers of this Testimony. Jesus is Lord. If anybody would meet me and ask me to say those words, I would be happy to say it to them.

I want to inform you a bit about my Scriptural knowledge journey. Starting as a child I was confirmed a Lutheran, so I learned the basics of Christianity. I did okay in school, but reading the Bible was a tough thing to do. As I aged into my 20s and 30s, I watched a lot of Pastors Joel and Victoria Osteen and Joyce Meyer and learned many things, but I was still inexperienced with sitting down and reading the Bible. I am telling you this because when I started experiencing God's power, I was not as experienced in reading the Bible as I should be at 43 years old. But you will see how God used that to my advantage.

One thing to know about this testimony is that out of respect for my family and friends, I will be leaving any negative information out of the story. Yes, it is true that it is part of the story, but there have been struggles that I choose not to disclose. That doesn't make the story any less true, it is just my private life as well as theirs.

Another thing that I must inform you about is that I will be intentionally not disclosing some miracles and, in some cases, entire periods of miracles due to my discernment telling me God does not desire it to be disclosed. I fear God and that is why.

Background

I grew up in Virginia. Son to a Pastor father and a second-grade Schoolteacher mother with an older sister and an older brother. My dad was a Pastor who believed God loves everyone and he taught me to look at each person as a valuable child of God. I started working around 13 years old as a paperboy for the local newspaper. I got up at 5:30 am, took a shower, and went to my stop to wait for the van to drop my papers off to deliver. I saved up for my first car with that job. During high school, I worked at a video store, a seafood restaurant, and a sub shop.

I started an instrumental band that lasted a couple of years. I played lead/rhythm guitar, and it has always been my passion. We were an original instrumental band. After the band broke up and I finished high school, I decided to try selling real estate. I worked hard and had some success. I bought three homes and life seemed successful in the real estate market dried up in Virginia which was because of the great recession. By this time, I had met my wife, Andrea, a few years before. This was unexpected and not an easy thing for us because we lost a lot of possessions and income.

We moved to South Florida. We each worked different jobs for a few years until we decided to go to college. I was going for an electrical engineering degree, and she was going for a nursing degree. Our schooling was cut short due to personal reasons, and we moved to Charlotte, NC.

We worked more jobs in Charlotte while ending college online. I went to Saint Leo University while Andrea went to The University of Phoenix. We both received associate degrees.

We then moved to the Eugene, Oregon area for two years. We then moved to Vancouver, Washington which is where the beginning of my journey with Jesus began.

I feel like I owe it to the readers to discuss my psychological health. In all fairness, you probably don't know me, and you are about to read about some astonishing events. We serve an astonishing God. The same God that parted the Red Sea is alive today. I know this for a fact.

I want to tell you first about the problems that I don't have. I have never hallucinated or seen something that wasn't there. I have never heard voices that were not there. I have a quiet and sound mind and I always think rationally. I do not have thoughts of harming people, nor have I ever harmed anyone. I have had thoughts of defending myself and my family, but nothing more. Since Jesus healed my soul in 2020, I no longer even have anxiety. On rare occasions I do, but usually, it goes away quickly instead of being a chronic problem.

Here are some things that I do have. I have a healthy mind, body, and spirit. I have a heart that is filled with love. All is thanks to Jesus. I will get into it when this transformation takes place in this book. I have always had an okay mind, body, and spirit, but when Jesus put His hand on me, I went to a whole new level of health, especially in my spirit.

With all of that said, I have had some problems with anxiety, depression, and mild mood issues. I have always been like the strong silent type, not complaining about every discomfort and just fighting through it by working or having some beer. I just took my medicine since I was about 19 years old every night and I didn't have to even think about it. Even though I took 50 seconds every night to swallow some pills, I was still able to live a fun life with a multitude of friends and family and it has never been a problem.

I used to be a bit of a worrier which stole a lot of my joy, but in the big picture, I have always been me. My medicine didn't change who I was, it just helped me to manage my mood. The doctors had misdiagnosed me in the beginning, and since then the core diagnosis has been bipolar II disorder. For those of you who don't know, bipolar II disorder is a mild mood disorder as opposed to bipolar I. With medicine, I never have had any problems. Bi-polar II is just a mood condition, it doesn't produce hallucinations, nor does it make people do bad things. Most bipolar people are highly intelligent. Many of them are the lawyers and doctors that you see today. And you would never know it.

Many people don't know that John F. Kennedy, Abraham Lincoln, and Winston Churchill all had a degree of bipolar like I do. They did okay. I saw an interview with a psychiatrist that wrote a book about how people with bipolar make good leaders because bipolar people have two strong attributes that come with the condition. Empathy and creativity. Creativity to come up with ideas to solve problems and empathy to care about people suffering. God takes what was meant for our harm and uses it to our advantage.

In this book, this is the last me I will address my condition. I am the same as everyone else except I need medicine to keep me from getting agitated or moody. My functions are the same as everybody else, so it is not relevant to the events that take place in this testimony. I have always been of sound mind. There have been some unnamed people in my life that have tried to prove otherwise, but when they tried, ultimately, they lost. I am not responsible for the actions, misdiagnoses, or accusations of other people. I am only responsible for my own actions, and I am responsible for telling the truth in this testimony of Jesus Christ. I know my truth. And this testimony describes the most important Truth,

Jesus Christ, the Truth, the Way, the Light. Praise God.

Seeking Jesus

When my wife and I moved to Oregon in 2016, we had already been unsuccessful at conceiving a child for 12 years. I need to tell you; that my wife and I were so sad and hurt by this. We had been living paycheck to paycheck since the great recession and we could not raise the funds for fertility treatments. My wife had felt like she was being punished because all that she had ever dreamed of was having a child. It wouldn't have even mattered if we were rich. A baby meant so much to her and to me as well.

We discovered the industry of delivering lost and delayed luggage in our own vehicles. We would go to the airport and pick up the bags, load them in our cars and drive them to the passengers' homes. Most of the time we just left it on their porch when it was the middle of the night. We would start at Eugene airport, plan our routes, and drive hundreds of miles. It was so enjoyable. Oregon and Washington are beautiful states to drive around. At the time, I was smoking cigarettes, so I would smoke, drink coffee, and listen to music in my favorite car all while driving into the forests, mountains, and beaches of the Northwest. Not a bad gig.

I started smoking around 16 years old. I tried to quit many times, but it was just too hard. I somewhat enjoyed smoking, but I could feel the Holy Spirit convicting me anytime I felt good about it. God was telling me that it is bad for me. When I was in my early 20's I asked God for an undisclosed request. I told him in return I would try my best to quit smoking cigarettes if He would give me this request. I was addicted so strongly I knew that it would be a lie to tell God that I would quit that day because I knew I couldn't do it. So, I said I would try. To my surprise, He gave it to me. There wasn't anything visual or audible from God, it was just that what I wanted worked itself out. So, a few weeks later I gave quitting a try. It lasted a day or two then I went back to smoking and I apologized to God and went about my life. I tried several times over the next decade or so but, I just couldn't beat it. I will get back to this subject later.

After driving for a few weeks or so, I decided that listening to music wasn't productive enough. 99.9% of the night I was driving so I could listen to anything I wanted. I had already been a listener of Pastor Joel Osteen since 2008 on Television. I decided to get Sirius XM and listen to his radio station. I began listening to his sermons, one after another, and learning as much as I could. I must have listened to every sermon he had ever preached. I would go back and forth between music and Joel, but I learned so many things about God as well as practical ways to handle the problems of life.

I drove from 2016 through 2018 at this point, so, I had a lot of knowledge about Scripture, but I still didn't read the Bible all the way through. But I gained a lot of different areas of knowledge. I decided I wasn't going to listen to new sermons, and I decided to start living the Word instead of hearing it all the time. We are called to be doers of the Word and not just hearers.

At this point, my faith in God was growing stronger. All the things that Satan had been reminding me of past mistakes and accusations were starting to become resolved. I learned that Satan would try to make me feel like I don't deserve God's goodness because of my sins. That's just not true. I am forgiven. We have all sinned. We all come up short of the Glory of God. Only Jesus Christ Himself could have a human body and live a perfect, sinless life. When we confess our sins, repent, and ask for forgiveness, Jesus will forgive our sins.

The Loss

So, my faith was strong, and I was starting to feel good then one day in May of 2018, my wife pulled me into the bathroom and showed me a pregnancy test with a big smile and said, "We're pregnant". We both began to weep with tears of joy. We were so overjoyed. We thanked Jesus over and over. I was on top of the world. My wife would no longer feel the misery of not being a mother. We were so happy.

Without getting into too many details, several weeks later, Andrea started to feel pain. We went to the hospital. They said she had a miscarriage. We were both so distraught. I was a shell of a man. Andrea was so sad. When I got home, I just fell face-first in the bed and didn't move for over a day. I cried harder than I ever had in my life. I just remember laying in the bed face down, remembering that Jesus would give me beauty for my ashes.

There were many struggles with members of my family that happened after the miscarriage, but I will not get into them specifically. But I will refer to these struggles as "the struggles".

So, a week went by, and we went back to work and tried to feel better every day. One night, I decided I was going to start reading the bible, little by little over the next several months. This period is where the supernatural occurrences started to unfold.

I must disclose that the supernatural events that have occurred I have not shared with anyone, with one exception. (I shared with my wife a miracle that occurred in Washington after we later moved to Orlando, Florida in 2020. And a few more miracles in 2023. She is a Catholic and a follower of Christ. She is just overwhelmed when she hears it, so I didn't tell her very much) (I told another family member one thing in hopes of leading that person to Christ also, but nothing in much detail)

I also need to disclose that some of the miracles in Washington may be out of order chronologically. However, it does not matter and is not important to the main true story. I assure you that it is not necessary to understand the story. Until now, (December 2023) I have not written anything down for different reasons, but these events were so powerful that I could never forget them. There were periods of miracles that had so many communications that it is possible that some memories are not currently in my mind.

The Supernatural

I went through many struggles in my time in Washington. I will not discuss them, but the struggles were what I needed for my seeds of greatness to come out that Jesus planted.

I learned that we could have harmful spirits that can try to attach themselves to us like anxiety and depression. I was standing in my kitchen, and I felt an overwhelming spirit of depression trying to take over me. It wasn't like anytime in the past. It was powerful. It felt like it would injure me if I let it. My faith had grown so strong that I decided I would cast out the demon. I started screaming "I cast you out demon in the Name and Authority of Jesus Christ!" I used all my spiritual strength and after doing this over and over for a couple of minutes, the spirit went away, and I felt the depression leave my body and I was relieved.

My faith was very strong at this point. I praised Jesus. I sat down and started reading my bible. And I opened it up and I was prompted to the scripture that said, "And John answered and said, Master, we saw one casting out devils in thy name; and we forbad him because he followed not with us." Luke 9:49 then Jesus replied, and Jesus said unto him, forbid him not: for he that is not against us is for us. Luke KJV 9:50

At this point, I feel the Bible is alive. I read through it in astonishment. I decided I was going to apply whatever Jesus said in red letters, in my life and obey. So, I read the scripture, King James Bible "But the hour cometh, and now is, when the true worshippers shall worship the Father in spirit and in truth: for the Father seeketh such to worship him. (John 4:23) I considered that this may be the night of Jesus' return because I was not educated in Revelation yet.

All I knew was when Jesus came again, that would be the end. I didn't know the things that would take place first. And here I think Jesus is talking to me in scripture. I'm frightened at this point. I could feel the fear of God in me.

So, I got in my car and I drove around looking for a sign. I called my wife and told her naively that it is possible that night was the night Jesus would return. She thought I was wrong, so I went home.

So, in a fearful mood, I went back to the Bible. I cannot remember every scripture that I read, but I know that after reading more, I came back to John 4:23 and I read another scripture that was about walking by faith.

So, I decided to walk by faith to a church nearby that had an illuminated Cross that towered over the area. I then read a scripture that said something like "I will control your mouth and they will not be able to say anything". (I can't find that in the bible currently). The next thing that happened was astonishing and scary. I began to speak uncontrollably around my empty house. I was of sound mind, but I was uncontrollably speaking in what I believe was Dean Martin's voice and Billy Graham's voice. I could not stop my lips from moving. Then after several minutes of this, it stopped. I was glad. I didn't know what to think of that. It was astonishing, but scary. God was preparing me for something soon.

So, I went back to the Bible and flipped the page and I was back at the same scripture about, Jesus Controlling my tongue." And "they will not be able to say anything."

And then the next scripture, then said Jesus unto Peter," Put up thy sword into the sheath: the cup which my Father hath given me, shall I not drink it? John 18:11 KJV. I thought, "What does this mean?" Then I realized that I always carried around a pocketknife and it was in my pocket. So, I obeyed Jesus and put my knife away.

I continued to read and this time I was prompted again to (John 4:23). This time I was sure in my naive mind that Jesus was coming that night. I started to head out the door and thought in my naive mind, my dogs could get left behind. I had no idea what I was doing. I was just obeying God.

So, I dressed warmly and put the leashes on the dogs, and started walking by faith to the church. I called my wife and told her to look up if she heard the trumpets sound. I was confused and walking by faith. I was just obeying God. It was a walk of faith, no matter how crazy it looked.

On the way to the church, my wife found me through tracking and picked up the dogs. I love my wife dearly, but she thought I was being crazy. And to most people, I probably did look crazy that night. So, she went home, and I kept walking to the church for the next 15 minutes, and out of nowhere two police cars pulled up behind me with their sirens blaring.

One officer got out and came up behind me and began frantically checking my pockets for a weapon. He checked my jacket pockets and my jeans. My knife was at home. They pushed me up a hill and stopped me as I said, "Do you even know who I am?"

At this point I knew what was happening, the "Sword" miracle already came to pass, and next was "the tongue". So, I prepared myself and said, "What is this all about?" They said, "Your family is worried about you that you're going to the church." They said the" Church is closed". I said, "I wanted to get communion" Then the officer said," I know, your family wants to know what's wrong with you?

Normally I would not know what to say to that, but in a split second, the Billy Graham-sounding voice took over my mouth and said angrily," What's wrong with me?? For wantin' to receive the bloodline of Jesus Christ?? Then said," You can receive it and you can receive it" to the two of the officers. Then the voice said, "People get persecuted for their faith all of the time, Officer."

When Jesus was speaking through me, I realized that they were just blankly staring at me the whole time. They could not say anything. That was the third miracle that came to pass with those officers that all took place in 3 minutes.

One officer went back to his car and the other one just stared at me not with anger, but with an astonished face for several minutes.

They let me go and I walked to the church. Knocked on the door, then went home.

Then I came back and started reading the bible and I immediately turned to the scripture, "How much then is a man better than a sheep? Wherefore it is lawful to do well on the Sabbath days." Matthew 12:12. I felt Jesus was telling me that I did well by bringing my dogs with me. At this point the Bible is completely alive and I turned to the Old Testament and began reading and the scripture I read was something about "He has shown reproach for his neighbors "Can't find it in bible currently. And He was saying how my destruction was coming. The more I read the more ominous it got.

As I continued to read this, I was terrified, I said out loud" No! I will correct that right now!" What I believed he was referring to was my conflict with some friends that led to some harsh words. So, I ran to my computer and immediately posted an apology on Facebook to any friends that I have had a disagreement with. I ran back to the kitchen lifted the bible and started looking through the Old Testament and it seemed like God was still angry, so I realized only Jesus can save me. So, I turned to the red letters in the New Testament and the first red letters I saw were "Whoa, I have never seen such faith!" When Jesus said that it was like I had a death sentence lifted off me. I was all in at this point. I believed everything. That is the only way to truly communicate with God. You must believe. I have searched the KJV and I cannot find these exact Words.

I was so astonished and relieved. You cannot go to the Father without first going to Jesus. The Most High God was speaking to me like texting and I had the Grace of Jesus. So, I immediately thought that maybe Jesus would come alive in the Davinci Painting of Jesus. So, I pulled up a photo of the painting on my phone. And I began to look in admiration with our creator and I began speaking to Jesus. I said something like, "It's revealed now, you can show me your face and speak to me" And I was on my knees and I kept talking to Him. I knew in my heart He would show me something. As I was staring at the painting, my eyes suddenly shifted to Right Hand of Jesus? It looked like He was gesturing holding a cigarette!" My eyes grew huge, and I realized that Jesus wanted me to fulfil my promise of quitting smoking. So, I jumped up and grabbed my pack of cigarettes, slammed them in the trashcan, and I said to Jesus with all of my heart, "I don't care if I have to lose my job, end up homeless, curled up in a ball, and starve to death under a bridge, I will never smoke another cigarette again."

So, I relaxed and sat down on my couch. I looked at the New Testament. And I decided to read Jesus' words out loud. As I got to the words in red letters, "I felt and heard a powerful tremor in the room and my body, which made my arms start to push the Bible away from me! As I looked at the next line in red letters as it was pushed away, Jesus said out loud with an echoed sound, "Behold, the Kingdom of God is within you". Which means The Kingdom of God is among you. Yes, I heard Jesus' voice out loud.

I saw a glorious spirit trail and it moved independently. What I can tell you is I was blown away with amazement as this was the first time that I truly experienced God's presence visually. From that moment on, I have never been the same. It looked kind of like a sparkling trail of magic in a Disney movie.

So, I started reading out loud again about 5 minutes later on the couch and suddenly, it was like my body got twisted into several different positions which felt like I was being thrown around in my seat kind of like by a Big Hand. It was like "The Flash" comic book character did a divine surgery on me. When Jesus stopped, I was left sitting in a twisted position with both arms out in front of me holding my bible open and my neck creaked at an angle. For two seconds I sat still, and my eyes looked at the page I was on and the first words I read were "There, now his heart is fixed" Not sure where or if that is in the KJV, and then it seemed like the page was having an inner conversation and the next line said, "How will he protect himself? And the next line said, "His truth will be his shield and buckler." All of the Words from God in this paragraph I cannot find currently. That is part of the miracle.

Then I stood up and my heart felt such a warm love and health in my heart that I had never felt. I would love it if I felt like that all the time. I feel good in my heart most of the time, but it doesn't feel strong like that day. Not only that, but my whole body also felt rejuvenated. Since that moment, I am completely healthy with not a particle of sickness throughout my body. I now live in divine health. In Heaven, we will feel this Love eternally, and better.

The first thing I read when I sat down again was a verse that I cannot find today that said, "Do not cut off thy seed". Maybe I was the one who had an infertility problem and not my wife. I flipped the page and the scripture. The next scripture I read was Matthew 18:5. "And whosoever shall receive one such little child in my name receiveth me." I started having tears of joy." The tears were rolling down my face. God was telling me that that the next time my wife and I try to conceive that we were going to have a baby.

So, the next time I saw my wife, I told her that God promised me that we were going to have a baby the next time we try. Right before we started, I told her, "Repeat after me, I receive this child in Jesus' name." and she said it.

Days later, my wife told me she was pregnant. She gave birth 9 months later. What are the odds? 16 years of trying to have a baby and that one time was the time. I had seen so many miracles at this point I was praising God and thanking Him all the time. I would listen to Christian music with tears of joy. I knew not only that we were having a baby, but the baby would be healthy. Because The Creator will be forming her Himself, just like He does for everyone.

Things calmed down for a while and after a week of not smoking, I knew I would never smoke another one. I began to have a craving. I decided to ask God if I could use vapor instead, I told him if He said no, I would not do it. After all, the promise I made to Him was about quitting cigarettes and not coffee, beer, or anything else. After I asked, I flipped the pages and stopped on red letters, Jesus' words were "You know thy things that bring you peace" (Not found in the bible today.) I took that as I know cigarettes don't bring me peace, but He will trust my judgment on what I think is reasonable.

Two things to learn from the cigarette subject; It is possible, for some people that God will not fully show up in your life until you fulfill your oaths to Him as per scripture. The second is that God is less concerned with your consumption habits than with your obedience to Him. He gave me permission to vape because I asked in humility and was willing to obey if He said no. God knew when I slammed my cigarettes in the trash that I truly repented and that's when He took things to a whole new level. In a matter of seconds after I truly repented. I do not recommend anyone to vape. It is not good for you. For most people it leads to smoking also. Everyone needs to determine if something is ok in moderation or if it is controlling your whole life.

I began to search the scriptures for Jesus to speak to me, but I learned that He would talk to me in due season. Over the last four years, much of the time He was silent. It seemed like when I needed Him the most was when He showed up. Plus, after He spoke to me, in some way, I needed time to train myself not to disobey by accidentally forgetting. I tend to forget some things. But I kept seeing the scripture John 16:23—"And in that day ye shall ask me nothing. Verily, verily, I say unto you, whatsoever ye shall ask the Father in my name, he will give it to you." The seed and promise started to take root.

My parents offered to help us move to Orlando while our Daughter was in the womb. Again, I was obedient, I asked God if I could move, I closed my eyes, flipped the page, and opened my eyes and in red letters, Jesus said, "Take up thy bed and walk" I was perplexed, and I looked at the next red letters and Jesus said, "Take up thy bed and walk.", then I was mesmerized and I looked at the next red letters, and Jesus said, "Take up thy bed and Walk?" I smiled and realized Jesus was saying, pack up your belongings and move to Orlando. Now I'm in full confidence and obedience mode.

We packed up a moving truck with my car on the back and moved to a house in Orlando, Florida. We settled in and we were so excited to meet our daughter. She was born in September of 2020. I had so many times that I burst into tears of joy about my daughter. I have never felt as much joy as I did at this point. I spent most of my time working and my free time studying the Word and watching preachers on TV.

I began thinking about the possibility of what the scripture John 16:23 meant, in that day, you will ask me nothing and The Father will give you anything you ask. How could that be? How will I ask the Father? I was ready for anything because I was in so much awe of what I experienced. Not only that I get full confirmation of His existence, but He showed up in my house and I saw, heard, and felt His power. As you can imagine, my mind has been overwhelmed with awe ever since.

There were many reasons that I kept all these things a secret. I knew what happened to people who witnessed Christ. I knew the first thing everyone would accuse me of is being insane or being a liar. Plus, during my times of reading live scripture, there was a scripture I read that told me not to share it. So, at this point I kept it secret, even from my wife. I wanted to get clear instructions from God on what He wanted me to do.

I began thinking about what I should ask for. Immediately I dismissed money, because just thinking about using my one request for money felt so greedy and evil. So, I began to think about positions, like the President of the United States. Not an evil request, but I believe God chose me because I don't desire to be powerful in a way that requires you to make tough choices, like war. God knows that I want to be a peacemaker and not responsible for fighting wars. I know that presidents can do a lot of good works, but it doesn't fit my nature. Then I started thinking about what really mattered. I searched my heart for one God-Sized request I could make for humanity. I thought, if I have an opportunity to receive anything, I thought it should be about the whole world instead of being just about me.

My heart was feeling that Jesus wants Salvation for His disobedient children so bad that He gives them chance after chance to repent. I was a man seeking God's heart.

I know that other people in scripture asked for wisdom and discernment. But I wanted to change the world. But I also realized I was going to be talking to The Heavenly Father Himself and I cannot ask for anything that conflicts with His Word. That made things a little tougher. I couldn't just ask for the whole world to be in heaven that day because that conflicts with scripture. I thought about asking for many different things, but finally I decided on asking God not to give any human soul that ever lived, living, or will ever live eternal punishment, including myself. I thought about how it would feel to know that some of our descendants or ancestors will be in eternal punishment while we are in eternal Light. I wasn't questioning God's justice or judgment; I was just going to plead a less harsh punishment for rejecting Him.

Scripturally, God is a sovereign God. Which means God's will is whatever God decides it to be. We do not tell God what to do. Nor can we. Think about the scripture, "I make known the end from the beginning, from ancient times, what is still to come. I say, 'My purpose will stand, and I will do all that I please.' Isaiah 46:10

The Father will do all that He pleases. Yes, He said that. He can change His mind anytime because He is perfect and He has the final say.

Think about when Moses pleaded with God to reconsider destroying His people. Moses was just a man, but God reconsidered and changed His mind, and spared His people.

I'm going to say this in all humility to any critics. Where is the harm in asking God for something like this? Does what I wanted to ask God affect you in a negative way or in a positive way? Do you think God will be looking at your heart if you are angered at such a compassionate act? The human soul is pure I believe. It is extremely valuable. I believe it is the sickness that accumulates in evildoers that is the problem. I believe only God's methods can purify a soul. The Catholics believe its purgatory, with God all things are possible. But I do believe God can purify any human soul and I believe; with God all things are possible. And I believe no one will enter The Kingdom of Heaven without repenting and accepting Jesus as their Lord and Savior. All souls must be purified to get into heaven. Jesus is the only Way to the Father.

So, at this point. I had decided. I would ask God for this.

The Request

It was either two or three days before Christmas 2020 when I was looking through scripture, I kept turning the page and seeing the Scripture about The one request of whatever I asked for from The Father. I was in the primary bedroom; my wife hasn't been sleeping in the same room with me for many years because I have a major snoring problem that keeps her up. She stays occasionally, but most of the time we have slept in separate bedrooms. It was raining heavily and it felt like God's presence was in the air. I cannot explain it, but due to the climate of everything that was going on in the world, and the thunderstorm, it felt like God's powerful presence was there.

So, I decided I would read some scripture out loud. In Washington, Jesus showed up in my house when I spoke out loud, so, I thought I would do it again. I got into the bed with my Bible. (Facing the headboard, I was on the right-hand side of the bed.)

I stirred up my faith. I opened near the Revelation location of the Bible. I looked at the two open pages before me. It appeared that the two pages were alive and moving. I looked to the top left of the left page and it said Revelation. Then the first Words at the top left page were, "Blessed is he who reads this out loud". I stared at this page and it began in the top left of the left page and it ended with a closing blessing in the bottom right of the right-hand page. The print on the entire two pages went back and forth between red and grey. I haven't found these two pages again at the present day. I read the whole thing out loud because I wanted to be blessed by Jesus.

As I looked at it, I felt Jesus' presence to my right very strongly. I cannot quote everything exact because I don't remember most of it. But here is what I do remember.

1. "Blessed is he who reads this out loud."
2. The first thing said was, "I have found one…." (I don't remember the end of that sentence)(In red letters)
3. Following not consecutive "I assure you, this one cannot bear evil."(Red Letters)
4. "We pray for the Lamb's Marriage." (Not in red letters) (It appeared like a conversation)

5. Then as I am reading this, My spirit began to become so strong and as I am reading it, as I read the red letters, next I read out loud" The Spirit is in me now" and I could feel something powerful and supernatural taking place in my spirit.

6. After that powerful experience, I looked at the next page and it looked powerful. I read it out loud, but I don't remember what it said because I had the fear of God in me and I struggled to even say it all. I had so much Godly fear in me, that it took all I had to get through the next page.

7. I do remember the final Word's in Red Letters were "God's grace to you all."

So, you can imagine, after I closed the book, I was in total Godly fear of Jesus in this moment. I had no idea what had just transpired. I just trusted Jesus. I slid over to the other side of the bed and was sitting up, and at this very moment, I could feel Jesus' presence again to the right of me, except this time I could sense a figure next to me with my eyes of faith. I couldn't see Jesus' face, but my eyes could just sense a silhouette and presence. And He said out loud faintly, "You did it" "Now you go to The Father." As Jesus said it, my spiritual eyes could see Jesus pointing up toward the sky as Jesus backed away." After Jesus said that I could sense a powerful presence in the sky outside of my house, but my spiritual eyes were able to see just for a second the silhouette of The Father God as He flew over my house. He was gigantic. I could sense His Power. I was frightened with Godly fear.

I realized that I hadn't asked Jesus for anything that day, which I usually do, so I knew this was it. I was going to the Father to make my request.

I got on my knees as I approached our Perfect Father, and said, "Father God, Praise you, I worship you, I love you with all of my heart, mind, and soul. Thank you for everything you've done for me. I come to you humble like a child, with no pride, with a pure heart, and in awe of you. I believe that Jesus has brought me to you today to request something" "I have thought about it and Jesus' two highest commandments are love The Lord your God with all of your heart, mind, and soul, and the second highest is Love thy neighbor as you love yourself" "So, that is what I am going to do. I am humbly with no pride asking for you not to send any human souls that have ever lived, are living, or will ever live to eternal punishment, including myself." "I know there are some wicked people out there, but I believe it is the devil's fault. The devil tricked them into becoming wicked." "I believe that with You, God, All things are possible. I believe that you can purify them.

I pleaded with tears rolling down my face, "if there must be justice and punishment that is your decision, but eternal torment, Father? That is just too much, Father. Remember when they were babies? You loved them then; they can be purified again. Do whatever you have to do, but please let them be saved through your Son Jesus Christ." "As for the wicked in the Spiritual realm that is your business, and you have said, "Vengeance is Mine" I am staying out of that war. Please do this for the ancestors that have children that have become lost, do this for them. I even asked him, "Impose Your Will if you have to, anything is better for them than eternal torment. I also ask if I am allowed to add something if that every animal's soul lives on in harmony." "I finished by saying," I ask you this Father in Jesus' name. Amen."

When I started, I was too scared to start a back-and-forth conversation with The Almighty Father, so that's why I just pleaded with my request and then waited for Him to reply. And as I sat there on the bed on my heels, a loud powerful voice boomed out, "Vengeance is mine" and I could see a silhouette of The Father flying away very powerfully. I was in awe as I slowly laid down on my bed. These last 20 minutes, I felt the Power of God. And as I laid there, I turned over on my side and began to ponder what The Father's words meant. Did He mean for the forces of darkness? And as I laid there, about four feet in front of me, out of another realm, the most glorious thing appeared.

It was a 5-foot Cross made of Solid Gold, adorned with large, precious, different color gems, and moving fire all around it. I looked in the other direction and looked back to strengthen my faith. It was there alright. It was so bright and real. Every detail from the rough surface of the gold to the sparkling gems, to the brilliant bright moving fire was marvelous.

And I wasn't scared. God has a way of making you at peace. I knew that Jesus was honoring me and saying" Your request is approved". I just stared in wonder and let it strengthen my faith. I would say it lasted in all its brilliant color for about a minute and then disappeared.

How could it mean my request wasn't approved? That wouldn't make sense. God doesn't give away awards for "nice try" or "close but no cigar". This was a deliberate symbol of excellence and beauty. As much as Jesus loves us for working hard and trying, He doesn't crown mediocrity. If my request was appreciated but not approved, He would not have revealed the symbol. He loves us all and he appreciates anything we do for Him, but what this symbol showed was the image of approval.

God wants me to make something perfectly clear. After hearing or reading about this Gift from God, do not commit suicide. God make the final decision, but if you commit suicide the punishment you will pay after suicide will be worse than if you just suffer waiting for your healing. Hang in there. Healing is coming.

Think about this, we can stop worrying. No one will ever be sentenced to eternal punishment all thanks to Jesus. All that I did was ask for this request in Jesus' name, God is in power. God did not need me to accomplish this. I will have to ask God why this all happened to me when I am in Heaven. Without Jesus, I am nothing. That is the real truth. And that goes for all of us.

Now, if you are a Christian mother or father and you have a child that has chosen atheism, worry not, your child will be found. Your child will be shown the Light.

During my time with Jesus, I didn't waste it. I got to know Jesus. I have to say, there were times that I was terrified. I had the realization that God is in my house and can show up anytime. I needed to rid myself of all impurities. Even impure thoughts. I had to become holy if I was going to be in the presence of God. Slowly Jesus removed my impurities, but I had to make a hard effort. I learned He wants to do works in us but we have to be willing to receive it. And we have to be willing to endure the pain of transformation. I knew then and I know now that what Jesus has to offer is far greater than we can imagine and even here on earth His ways are higher than the world's ways.

To the Christians of the world, I know this may seem shocking to what you have believed your whole life. You have to put it in perspective, God gave us warnings and promises in scripture. Most of the bible is warnings and promises. He has never broken a promise. He has decided to lessen the punishment. That means He had mercy on the warning of eternal punishment. His promises, He will never break. I will obey God no matter what his decisions are and I always have. Maybe God chose me because of my empathy. Jesus planted the seed of compassion in my heart, so He knew what I would ask for. Jesus orchestrated everything from the beginning until He pointed to the sky and said "Now, you go to the Father". This was God's plan all the way. I give all Praise and Glory to God, I am just so thankful to be fortunate enough to be a part of it.

You have to remember; that God is a sovereign God and He will do "All He pleases". For a reason unknown to me, He chose me to be one of the few in history to have the opportunity to receive anything I asked for. That in itself opened the door for The Father to change His mind. The Father never lied in scripture. There is nothing false in Him. However, He is allowed to change His mind. No one can tell God that He cannot change His mind. And He has made clear in scripture that He can change His mind when He said "I will do all that I please."

God taught us everything we know about the Divine through scripture, but He didn't teach us everything He knows. There are so many secrets of the universe that God did not put in scripture. Think about it, this adds to His Glory. He agreed to eliminate the harshest of harsh punishments. I begged for this on my knees for all of you. I begged for people of different faiths, people with no faith, and all people to be given the opportunity of purification because after we leave this world, we will leave this all behind.

Remember this scripture, 2 Peter 3:9
King James Version

9 The Lord is not slack concerning his promise, as some men count slackness; but is longsuffering to us-ward, not willing that any should perish, but that all should come to repentance.

It has never been God's will for any of us to perish, but that all should come to repentance. So, by not perishing any soul, God is keeping His will. And by keeping His other mysterious methods as a way to bring every soul to repentance, He is further keeping His Word.

The thing I need to point out is that the only thing God has changed is removing eternal punishment. I don't think it would be a good idea to be outraged at that. The amount of mercy we show others is the same amount of mercy we will be given, so I advise everyone to just receive it and thank The Father, The Son, and The Holy Spirit for this Astounding, Marvelous, Merciful, Beautiful, and Wonderful Gift! Hallelujah!

Jesus Saves

After the request, things settled down and many things happened in my life that I won't get into. I experienced some trials that led to miracles that I will not mention. I began training to become a truck driver. I got a commercial driver's license and started driving for a fuel tanker delivery company. What happened next was incredible. I was on the last day of my training as a driver and my trainer gave me a truck to follow him in. Before I started, I was nervous. This was the first time I was driving a tractor-trailer alone.

I started leaving out of the yard and I approached the exit. There was a gate and a large ditch approximately five feet deep and approx. 15 feet wide directly to the right side after you exit the gate. I never thought about it because my trainer always made me exit to the left. I got to the exit and slowly went up to the street. It is a two-way-two total lane street. I noticed my trainer had just turned ahead of me and I panicked because I felt like I had to stay behind him. There was a car stopped right in front of me on the opposite side of the street. So, I made a foolish mistake. I turned in the right lane without waiting for traffic to clear to turn in the oncoming lane for the needed turning space to stay out of the ditch. Dumb move. I should have rolled the whole truck over into the ditch.

I basically turned a tractor-trailer like an SUV without any extra turning space. As I turned, the first thing I heard was a loud bang and I looked back through my day cab window and saw the gate getting ripped off and after I stared back at it, I looked forward and noticed that my foot was flooring the accelerator. Something told my spirit to stay still and the next thing I realized is that I was on the road perfectly straight. Not only that, but there was just a small dent on the toolbox on the passenger side of the trailer when I pulled over. It defied the laws of physics.

I realized that I prayed to God before I drove by myself that He would take control over my body if I was going to hurt myself or someone else. Jesus saved me again. Praise God.

I later got let go of this job and they did a review of me and the safety manager with many years of experience said in amazement, "I have studied the site where the incident happened over and over, and I cannot see how you didn't roll that trailer into the ditch. "I thought to myself, Jesus, that's how." Praise God.

The Choir

Around the time of the rescue of my life in my truck, I was at my house with my family one day. My wife invited her friend and daughter over. We had two living rooms. Everybody was in one room; I went into the other room. We had a little 2" smart speaker in the kitchen that was playing some music, but the kitchen was so far away I could barely hear it.

Most of the time you don't fully understand what is happening the second things happen with God. I was sitting there and all of a sudden I realized that I was surrounded with loud singing. Then in the last few seconds I realized it sounded just like a church Choir. It was a Choir of Angels. They were surrounding me. It was beautiful and it made me feel holy in my whole body. It sounded as loud as ten Bose systems with perfect clarity. I looked and no one in the other room could hear it. Then they quieted down. I was astonished. Yet, I never told anyone. I have been waiting for God to tell me if or when to tell anyone.

Because of all of the hell we went through, my wife and I have decided to divorce. We fought so hard to keep it, but my marriage put us through so much we feel more like warriors than lovers. This is my private life, so I will not be sharing anything negative about my marriage. But my wife was an amazing supporter of mine many times, so she will always be under God's protection as she already is as well as my daughter and I are. Our divorce is not only approved by God, it is encouraged.

The Most Astonishing

In January 2023, my wife noticed that the carpet was wet in our living room. Water was leaking from the back of the house. We eventually got it tested for mold. The kitchen, living room, and HVAC system all had high levels of black mold. In the weeks after having it tested my daughter began to cough badly. Then my wife and I got sick. We went to the doctor two or three times. We were taking antibiotics, but it just wouldn't go away.

During our illness one night, I was laying in my bed in a mostly dark room, on my left side facing the middle of the bed and I was just resting, and I began to laugh about a joke that I thought up and as I was laying there laughing, I saw a Light begin to form on the other side of the bed. As I focused I saw Jesus powering up the mystical power of His Hand like He was going to fire it at me. It appeared like He was in another realm. I got scared and humbled myself and closed my eyes and put my head down and called out," Yes Jesus, yes Jesus, I'm Sorry" So, I looked up and Jesus was still there with His illuminated hand, and that second, He fired it at me. It was like a fast 12" wide beam and it went straight to my torso. The thing was, it felt like pure Love and it felt so good. I looked at my torso as it hit me and looked back and His face was partially in a shadow and He Stood up and backed away. He was wearing what looked like His King's Attire. The King of kings' attire. The next second, it looked like He had changed into more casual clothes and I could see His full Being move away what appeared 25 feet or so to His right. He had a straight face the whole time until, t very end it looked like He gave me a kind smile and then disappeared.

The smile made me feel His kindness and gentleness. His smile meant more to me than anyone will ever know.

The next day, I got up and was drinking coffee or something and I realized, my lungs were clear. I was no longer sick. I realized that my wife and daughter were not sick either. I asked my wife and she was not sick nor was my daughter. The Divine Physician had healed again. Up until that morning, I had no idea what Jesus fired at me and why. I went from coughing nonstop and feeling weak as well as my whole family to waking up as healthy as ever. I love Jesus so much. When He does something, He does it awesome.

I daydreamed about seeing Jesus again for the next day. The next day, I was lying in almost the same position and I wasn't expecting it, but another sight appeared in front of me. As it came clear, I got a full view of Jesus standing in His Glory staring at me with a straight Face. His hair was long and His face was almost identical to His Face in the "Davinci's Jesus" Painting. He was holding His hands down in front of Him, holding something Illuminated. I am not sure, but it appeared like He was standing on an empty planet in another realm like the moon or another. There were big rocks behind Him. His background was not lit, but He was. It appeared that each face of Jesus had differences than the previous or He could just have a face that looks different in different attire. I am not sure. I just waved to Him as He disappeared.

After about 20 seconds, the realm shifted to Jesus wearing light color clothes as He sat with His eyes closed for about 5 seconds then He disappeared. Maybe Jesus was telling me to pray more. This was around March or April of 2023. Praise the Father, Praise the Son, and Praise the Holy Spirit.

The rest of this book is devoted to carrying out God's Will. Yes, I have had other encounters with God, but God has called me to tell the world that God is calling for peace in 2024. God is being as productive as possible with me and I am here at His request.

Jesus is the Answer to the World's Problems

I pray for peace in this world. I pray men put down their weapons and solve problems in different ways. I pray for every man, woman, and child to learn that Jesus loves every single one of you and He died for your sins. Jesus has already paid the price for your sins. I pray you now accept His gift of Salvation, and praise His Wonderful Name and see that The Father Loves Him. I pray this in Jesus' precious and kind name, Amen.

I never dreamed I could have been taken on a journey on earth with the True and Living God in this way. He has given me protection, peace, joy, a baby, and so much more. I know that as long as I love God with my whole heart, mind, and soul, He will continue to bless me. And it is my great joy to do so. As the scripture Luke: 24 says in King James Bible; "For I tell you, that many prophets and kings have desired to see those things which ye see, and have not seen them; and to hear those things which ye hear, and have not heard them."

It is not proven that we are in the end times right now. I believe every word in the bible. The way I think my request to God fits in with Revelation is that Jesus holds the pen on who is written in The Lamb's book of life. With that said, Jesus can save any soul in existence with His pen.

I consider myself very blessed and gifted by Jesus. I have always put Him first place and I always will. I know God's heart and He is humble at heart and rich in mercy.

There are some things that can be verified in my story like the police vehicle camera that was facing me the whole time when Jesus took control of my speech. Also, my former employer can be interviewed about how it was not physically possible for me to make that turn in the tractor-trailer without rolling it into that ditch. I am not going to put a lot of energy into proving my honesty because I know that God will make the truth be known in some way.

For new believers of Christ, especially in violent countries, you don't even need to go to a place of worship and endanger yourself. You can pray in secret. Matthew 6:6 "But thou, when thou pray, enter into thy closet, and when thou hast shut thy door, pray to thy Father which is in secret; and thy Father which seeth in secret shall reward thee openly."

I pray that everyone and their families can be at peace knowing that they will be in the presence of all of their loved ones in heaven and they can be at peace with their neighbors, enemies, and brothers and sisters. Just know Jesus literally felt every pain you felt when He suffered on the Cross. He went through it all to show you that He didn't want you to think that He was sitting on high watching everyone suffer, instead He felt every pain you felt in your life as He humbled Himself as a man. So you cannot blame or be angry with Jesus, He felt every injustice that you experienced yourself. He did it because He wanted each and every one of you to know that you are not alone in your suffering. Now that is the greatest gift in life. And that gift is Jesus. In order for the human race to become what it will become, we first need to understand God's Love. When we trust God, we all win.

To the World, I know there are many different religions here on earth, but I am here to tell you that I am a witness of God and I have witnessed His Glory and Jesus Christ is the True and Living God. Christ is the only way. Why is Jesus the only way? Because He says so, and He is the Truth. There is nothing false in Him. I don't claim to understand everything and I can't explain why God allowed there to be so much confusion about God. All that I can say is I have seen Jesus with my very own eyes. I have felt His powerful healing power like a beam of love on my torso. And so much more. I am no longer just an American. I am no longer of this world. I speak as a representative of the Most High God in existence. The God who tells the mighty oceans to calm. The God who sends comets on their path. The God who feeds all of the animals, birds, and fish all with zero effort. Everything God does is with zero effort. There is nothing too hard for God.

As I try to understand how this confusion started, I can't help but think of the story of the tower of Babel in Genesis. The people of the earth were rebelling against God by building a tower to Heaven. Everyone was united in this rebellion. That is when God split up the people and I believe that is when the races were created and different languages as well. There was a reason for that. I believe that since God's children acted together against God, He decided to give us our own problems and now we would need to go to Him for rescue.

As regarding Christian, Islam, and Jewish relations. The first thing to acknowledge is that we are all descendants of Abraham. Therefore, the God of Abraham is our God. Islam calls The Father Allah, Christians and Jews call The Father Jehovah and Yahweh. The name we call The Father doesn't change who He is. He is the same Father of Creation. There is only one Father God.

Long before the Prophet Mohammed was born, The Father decided to save the world from our sin. The only way this could be achieved was to send His only Son, Jesus, to be transformed into a Human through the Blessed Mother Mary by the Holy Spirit conceiving his Being and then as an adult, be crucified and pay the price for every one of our sins and rise three days later. Without Jesus, none of us could be forgiven. Jesus is the Savior of the world. Jesus is Fully Human and Fully God simultaneously.

Although many people adored Jesus, there were some Pharisees that rejected that God had a Son. Why? Because it was not written in the Old Testament. There are over 300 prophecies in The Old Testament that Jesus fulfilled in His first coming. But just because Jesus wasn't specifically mentioned as God's Son, they rejected the idea.

Although Jesus had enemies that were Jewish, He had many Jews that loved and adored Him. Jesus loves everybody. Jesus even loves the Pharisees that sought His death. And He doesn't just love the Pharisees because they were part of His plan to save the world. I say again, Jesus loves everybody. Jesus can see past the wickedness in any person and see the true person of love that they can become. Jesus doesn't think like we do here on earth. We are taught to take revenge and balance out the scales. Jesus is only interested in the end result of things.

 Maybe that's why He chose me to be one of the few people in history to be given the opportunity to ask the Father for anything in Jesus' name and receive it. All I had to do was ask in Jesus' name. I could be the richest man in the world right now if I asked, but I valued the souls of (In no particular order) the Asians, the Indians, the Africans, the Arabs, the Spanish, the Jews, the Caucasians, unbelievers, criminals, blasphemers, and everyone else more than my own comforts. This is hard to believe for many I'm sure, but I testify that every word in my testimony is true. But I give all of The Glory to God for this miracle. Jesus knew what was in my heart because He put it there. Without God, I am nothing, but with God I am an eternal being.

With that said, Jesus is of Jewish blood. The Father chose Mary as His Mother. The Jews are God's chosen people. The Father loves His chosen people in a special way. His Son Jesus is Jewish. The good news is The Father loves each tribe in a special way as well. God has an infinite amount of love to spread around. If you are of the Islamic faith, you may ask why so many Jews reject Jesus. It is written in scripture in the New Testament Romans 11:25 "For I would not, brethren, that ye should be ignorant of this mystery, lest ye should be wise in your own conceits; that blindness in part is happened to Israel, until the fullness of the Gentiles be come in."

As soon as the fullness of the "Gentiles" (Which is anybody other than a Jew) come to Christ, the Jewish people will have "The veil" removed by the Father and they will see the overwhelming evidence of Christ.

I am saddened for the Jewish people for all of the persecution they have endured. The Father will never and never has forsaken them. His plans are perfect. God bless the Jewish people for being part of God's plan to save the rest of the world. The Jewish people lived such a hard role in God's perfect plan to save all of our souls. Some thanks are in order to God's chosen people.

To the people of Islam, the world wants peace. I am not a political historian, but it seems that sometime in the past, violence occurred between some nations, including Islamic nations that left painful wounds, that sparked retaliation. Which sparked more retaliations and so forth until we are where we are today. I am a Christian, and I want you to know, I feel your pain. I could never feel your pain to the extent that you have felt. And for the losses of your loved ones, my heart goes out to you. I have expressed my love for Israel and Jesus, but I want to embrace every one of you as a brother and sister and say, I love you. It's time for love to have the upper hand. Let's end this madness and let the soldiers go home to their families. Family is what truly matters.

For those of you that don't know. Jesus sits at the Right Hand of the Father in Heaven, and one of His names there is "The Prince of Peace". Even though He is peaceful, He is All-Powerful. This is the thing humans never understood. Waging war doesn't show your power, it shows your weakness. Jesus is in the highest position of power, yet He remains at peace. Until you submit to peace, you cannot have power. Maybe the world's economies will improve if we stop destroying it.

The United States of America is a peaceful country. When America goes to war, it is to fight injustice. No nation is perfect, but America is built as one nation under God. When America has gone to war, it is to stop evil forces from taking over the world, such as WWII. America is a protector to smaller nations that cannot protect themselves from brutal takeovers. America has a long history of giving food, provision, water, and disaster relief to the hurting of the world. America has been an ally of any God-fearing nation that looks to help the world and not destroy it. God loves America also because 90% of the Gospel spreading comes from the United States.

America does not want any further conflict with the people of Islam. I say this because it is a known fact. The American people want the world to be at peace. Christianity and Judaism are peaceful religions and any conflict with Islamic nations have been retaliations of bloodshed and not an attack against your Islamic religion. I can tell you with certainty that The God of Abraham would not allow me to say that if it wasn't true.

God's Call for Peace

I have shared many ways that I have communicated with God in this book. But there are some ways that I communicate with God that I will keep to myself. With that said, I have had clear communication from God that He wants to see peace in the world THIS YEAR 2024. He wants the wars to end THIS YEAR 2024. I do not know what else will happen, but over and over again God has told me all wars need to cease THIS YEAR (2024).

To President Putin, if you are reading this you may be asking, who is Steven Nelson to tell me what to do? It's not Steven Nelson calling for peace Mr. Putin, It's the King of Kings, Jesus Christ. He is calling for you to end the wars. Yes, I have met Him in my house. I have even had the Father God Himself come to my house and offer me anything I asked in Jesus' name. If you ask me what did I do to deserve this goodness from God, I will have to say, it's a gift. Throughout scripture, God chose the most unexpected and overlooked people. I am no exception. I am not wealthy, famous, or powerful in my own strength. My strength is in God. Mr. Putin, you know how you meet with Ambassadors from other countries? Well, I am an Ambassador for Heaven. And I have been instructed to send the message to you that God wants Peace in the world THIS YEAR (2024). Think about this Mr. Putin, this is not Mr. Biden or Mr. Trump calling for this, it is God Himself. And make no mistake, God is on the Throne. The sooner the better. He specifically stressed THIS YEAR. And God is not singling you out, Mr. Putin, He wants all of the wars in the world to end THIS YEAR (2024). It's time to go the negotiating table.

God will extend a grace period to April 15th 2025 if Donald Trump will meet with Steven K. Nelson before election.

To Israel, I have a direct connection to The God of Abraham. You call Him El Shaddai. God has so much love for you, Israel. It's time to negotiate for peace. God bless you.

To Hamas and Iran, you call The God of Abraham, Allah. I have seen the God of Abraham and I have spoken to Him. He chose me, Steven Nelson, a modest man, to relay the message that there must be peace this year (2024). At first, I thought that God just wanted me to share my encounters and share the gift of the eventual purification of every soul with the world. But God is very persistent with me that He wants world peace this year (2024). It's time to negotiate for a peaceful resolution.

To any other Islamic organization with war on their minds, we are all descendants of Abraham, therefore brothers and sisters. Your God does not want any more innocent bloodshed. We all must obey The God of Abraham. Islam is not an exception. I am obeying God by writing this. This is not my independent mission. This mission comes directly from The God of Abraham and His Son, Jesus Christ.

It is time for all nations with tensions to go to the negotiating table. Everyone has something and everyone wants something. A desire to steal your neighbors land and resources is not a just cause. Everyone needs to swallow their pride and negotiate for a peaceful resolution to your conflicts. If you come to a peaceful resolution with your neighbor, your nation will be blessed by God. God had me send you that promise. You have just been offered a "Promise" from God for each nation that makes peace with their enemies.

Think about that. That is one of the biggest miracles in this book. The Most High God is promising each nation that makes peace with their enemies that their nation will be blessed by God. Peace is a blessing by itself, but you will get your whole nation blessed by God if you make peace. And as you know, God never has broken a promise. We as humans do, but God never does.

Let me speak from the heart to the world. I just see myself as a normal guy from Virginia. I don't see myself as this Celestial Angel who hovers over his seat with a halo over my head. Before January 2020 I was in the same boat with God as everyone else, looking up at the stars just wishing that God would reveal anything to me. I never understood why we had to live our lives without seeing God because we all love Him so much. I was searching for my sign my whole life.

Before January 2020 I was battling physical problems, especially in my heart from smoking. My marriage was struggling because we just could not conceive a child. Ever since the great recession, I just could not make it financially again. I had friends and family turn their backs on me. I felt like I bet everything on my wife because she bet everything on me. We were in the darkest days of our life. Then Jesus showed up and changed everything in a day.

So, no. I don't feel like I am so much better than anyone else. One of the reasons I believe God chose me is because I learned how to be virtuous. I learned the only way to fight a sin is with a virtue. And pride is one of the worst sins. To combat pride, you need humility. And to be in the presence of God, you need humility.

To tell you the truth, I don't even like to pat myself on the back for good things that I accomplish with God because too much self-esteem leads to selfishness. When I honestly look at what I did, I can see that it was a world-changing request to God and it makes me happy that God is happy with me. But I have to leave it there. There is no room in heaven for a prideful heart or a big head. We are all valuable to God. I am not loved by God more than anyone else. Yes, He may be pleased more with me than some, but in Heaven, He will be pleased with everyone.

God honors people in heaven. He even gives crowns to some. He is my King. He is my Savior. He is the reason I am alive. I will worship Him forever and serve Him forever as His most grateful, joyful, and loving servant.

But even the person in Heaven with the least reward will have such a reward that they will be fulfilled by the Light eternally. There will be no sorrow. There will be no pain. Being in Jesus' presence is all anybody will ever need. As scripture says, God is Love. Love is Divine. And one of the best parts about making it to heaven is that we will no longer have the knowledge of evil. Just like in the Garden of Eden before Adam and Eve ate the apple, they had no knowledge of evil. I can't wait for humanity to get back to Eden again. I want it so bad; I think about it all the time.

So, no, I don't think of myself as a big shot trying to make world peace. I have actually been so nervous communing with God, making sure that I don't say something wrong I have felt in shock for weeks. No, God is not mean, but He is putting an enormous amount of trust in my ability to discern His Will. Which is a big responsibility.

I have not said anything offensive in this book. Informing the world that God wants world peace and no more innocent bloodshed should not be offensive to anyone. Imagine what the world could be like if everyone just worked in a trade and came home for dinner with their families. Even in poor countries, most people there would love to work hard every day if they could just have an abundance of food, clean water, and savings for retirement, and a safe home without the terror of war. I think if the world would invest in the labor and development of poor countries by creating jobs, the world would be surprised how hard they will work and how much farther a charitable dollar would go. Most people just want the same things that new world countries have. I think a better way to handle the migration problems is to rebuild these countries by giving the citizens the tools and training to get it done and compensate them.

So, no, I don't think I'm a big shot. I am not any more valuable than you. However, I am representing the world's creator. I can downplay myself, but I don't and I won't downplay God. He flung the stars into place. He knew you before He formed you in your mother's womb. He stole the keys to death and hell. He is an Awesome God. And most importantly, He knows your heart. You are His holy child. There is nothing Jesus wouldn't do for you to win your heart.

Just for some peace of mind for you: The Anti-Christ in Revelation will require everyone to worship himself and proclaim himself as God. I want you to Worship Jesus Christ directly in Heaven and I am not God. I have the Spirit of Jesus in me just like Pat Robertson, Joyce Meyer, Billy Graham, Joel Osteen and countless other Pastors say. Every Believer has the Spirit of Jesus in them; however, He is just very strong in me. He and i demand that you do not bow to me. The Anti-Christ will require you to bow to him. Not me. I'm not saying that anybody would bow down to me. I am just trying to ease the anti-Christ fears. A friendly wave would be fine, but you are not required to do anything for me, just for Jesus. Look at me, I have only an associate degree and I cracked the code that no one fully understood. It's because Jesus' Spirit is with me and in me. Billy Graham said everyone has a God-given soul, but His spirit can only dwell in your temple if it is whole. I'm not saying you have to be perfect, but you need to desire His Spirit in your temple and seek after it with all your heart mind, and soul because your spirit is what communes with God. That is the complete opposite of what the Anti-Christ is prophesied to be. I am not the false prophet either because the false prophet will tell everyone to worship the Anti-Christ, and I am leading everyone to the Risen Savior, Jesus Christ who is in heaven. It doesn't take many seminary courses to see that the Anti-Christ wouldn't say this. Jesus is Lord.

I hope the world could listen to these favorite songs of mine in order. These Stars and their harmless supporters have all been appointed by God. Including NATO, Taylor Swift's Cause. The Church of Christ (All Churches that worship Jesus Christ), and Israel. Peaceful nations can join anytime. All are welcome to lay down your weapons and join our peaceful alliance of nations after World Peace is achieved. Rules can be agreed on later. This Mighty Army of God shall not be touched. The following list are under the Protection of Almighty God. Ezekiel 25:17 KJV--- I confirmed this with God many times. Here are some of my greatest Heroes. If you become our friend, and make enemies, then they would become our enemies and most importantly, God's enemies. And then they would fear you. (It is what it is.) Our war is not against flesh and blood, God will execute great vengeance with furious rebukes. A rebuke is a strong punishment but not death. And if you experience these rebukes, you will have no doubt He is the Lord. If you don't want rebukes, just don't do it. Just let it be peaceful and pray for peace. God has told me, he desires mercy. The reason God has not acted yet in these wars is because we have freewill. Now He has revealed the true meaning of Revelation. It's all in Jesus' Pen and Book of Life. He would rather end it by writing everyone's name in the Lamb's Book of life. Jesus is not expecting you to stop sinning perfectly, He just wants your heart first. What more could you ask for? And it has a silver lining. God is an Awesome God indeed.

If Everyone Cared- by Nickelback

Believe- by Lenny Kravitz

Rescue Story- by Zach Williams

There was Jesus- by Zach Williams, Dolly Parton

Jesus wrote me a letter- Baylor Wilson

Peace- by We the Kingdom and Bethel Music (I listen to this when I need peace)

The Blessing- by Bethel Music, We the Kingdom

Waking up- by We the Kingdom

What a Beautiful Name- by Hillsong Worship

King of kings- by Hillsong Worship

Battleborn- by The Killers (Amazing beings of Faith)

Imagine- by John Lennon

Firework- by Katy Perry

Cinderella Man- By Rush

Cinderella Man –by Eminem

I have seen the way-(Alex Lifeson, Kirk Hammett & Dr. Fresch)

Pull me under—by Dream Theater

Pneuma – By Tool

Descending – By Tool

Selah-by Kanye West

Now We Are Free---Gladiator Soundtrack---Songwriters: Hans Zimmer / Klaus Badelt / Lisa Gerrard

One Day- by Matisyahu

Working them Angels- Rush

The Angel's Share- by Geddy Lee

My Hero-by the Foo Fighters

The Pretender-by the Foo Fighters

Clockwork Angels-by Rush

Cygnus X-1 Book I- by Rush

Cygnus X-1 Book II Hemispheres- By Rush

The Veil-by We the Kingdom

No doubt about it- by We the kingdom

God is on the Throne- by We the Kingdom

Count the Stars (Be there for you)—By We the Kingdom

Blessed Be the God of Israel- by Lutheran Hymn Project

Take it all Back- by Tauren Wells, We the Kingdom

Crazy in Love-by Beyoncé, Jay-Z

Raise your glass-by Pink

Toxic- by Britney Spears

Like I love you- by Justin Timberlake

(Second Wave)

Tennis Court- by Lorde

Larger than life-by Backstreet Boys

This I promise you- by NSYNC

Ain't that a kick in the head-by Dean Martin

Uptown Girl- by Billy Joel (All of your songs are copyrighted in your name now)

Touch of Grey- by the Grateful Dead

My Sweet Love- by George Harrison

How deep is your love-by Bee Gees

Good Good Father- by Chris Tomlin

Remembrance- by Bela Flek

Stayin' Alive- by Bee Gees

Something's gotta give- by Sammy Davis Jr.

Take me on a ride- by We the Kingdom

End of the line- by Alex Lifeson

It's been Awhile- by Stained

Wonderful place/Waiting for you—By N.E.R.D

Neal Peart's Family—Rest in peace, Neal.

Closer to the Heart (live)—by Alex Lifeson

Human Race- by Rik Emmett

Tighten Up- by the Black Keys

Bravest face-by Rush

Waiting on the World to Change---by John Mayer

Closure- by Chevelle

Shine- by Collective Soul

Have you ever seen the rain-Creedence Clearwater Revival-

Textures- by Cynic

The Heart of Life—by John Mayer

Emoji of a Wave-(Wave Two)--- Another piece of Genius by John Mayer

Free Fallin' --John Mayer Live at the Nokia Theatre, Los Angelos, CA

Why you no love me- by John Mayer (Peace to Asia)

Tai Shan- by Rush (Peace to China)

Dreaming of you – by Selena (Peace to Mexico)

Totem- by Rush (Look up to the Most High, He loves all of you) (The Holy Trinity is the Most High God, But there are many Gods in the Universe)

Red Sector A- by Rush Live in Rio (The Love of Rush in Brazil shows they see the light) God Bless you Brazil.

What makes you beautiful-by One Direction

Give me a sign- by Breaking Benjamin

The Pass- by Rush Live in Rio

Dream Dealer- by Chad Hugo

Greg Again Playlist- by Greg Placides

Paint it, Black- the Rolling Stones

Born in the U.S.A.- By Bruce Springsteen

Weight of Sound-by Stick Figure

When it's Love—by Van Halen

Right Now—By Van Halen

Who Says-By John Mayer

It was a very good year-by Frank Sinatra

Something – by the Beatles

Let it be- The Beatles

Here comes the sun- by the Beatles

Innocent—by Taylor Swift (Repent to Jesus and this will be everyone's song)

Anti-Hero- by Taylor Swift (A True Goddess of Light and an Inspiration to all of Creation)

Mastermind--- by Taylor Swift

Hey Stephen (Taylor's Version)- by Taylor Swift (Hey, a guy can dream right? lol)

Romeo and Juliet- by the Killers

Come fly with me- by Frank Sinatra

Daylight- by Taylor Swift

I'd die for you- by Bon Jovi

Fear is Liar- by Zach Williams

What's left of me-by Nick Lachey

Let it Go-by Idina Menzel

Into the Unknown-by Idina Menzel

For the First Time in Forever-Kristen Bell, Idina Menzel

Shake it off-by The Smashing Pumpkins

Get Along---by Kenny Chesney

Hysteria – by Def Leppard

Eric Johnson- by Cliffs of Dover

My Own Summer- by Deftones

Fear Inoculum- by Tool

Like a Prayer- by Madonna

Ray of Light- by Madonna

Change- by Michael Jackson

Bad-by Michael Jackson

The Way you make me feel- by Michael Jackson

Feel the Pain-by Dinosour Jr.

Tommy the Cat- by Primus

Riders on the Storm- by the Doors

Numb- by Linkin Park

Bad Decisions- By Benny Blanco, BTS, and Scoop Dog)

WE are the Champions- by Queen

Hotel California- by the eagles

Tranquilize- by the Killers, Lou Reed

Wonderful tonight-by Eric Clapton

Sugar we're going down- by Fall Out Boy ☺

Basket Case- by Green Day

Dig- by Incubus

Never Tear Us Apart- by INXS

Carolina in my Mind-by James Taylor

Superhero-Janes Addiction

N 2 Gether Now- by Limp Bizkit, Wu Tang Clan

South of Heaven- by Slayer (This gift is for all Humans) (Don't worship the Imagery) (It's a disguise)

Death Certificate- by Carcass (and all metal bands that Geddy Lee vouches for)

Acid Rain- Liquid Tension Experiment

Sweet Home Alabama-by Sweet Home Alabama

Poker Face-by Lady Gaga

Body and Soul- by Tony Bennett

American Girl- by Tom Petty and the Heartbreakers

Sail on- by Tommy Emmanuel

Beer for my Horses- by Toby Keith

So What – by Miles Davis

Lover of the Light- by Mumford and Sons

Hurt- by Nine in Nails

Burn- by Norah Jones

Wonderwall- by Oasis

Do I wanna know? –by Artic Monkeys

Walk- by Pantera

Misery Business- by Paramore

Dark Side of the Moon Album- by Pink Floyd

Waste No Time-by Passafire

FourFiveSeconds by Rihanna, Kanye West, Paul McCartney

Live your Life—by T.I., Rihanna,

Young, Wild, & Free (Feat. Bruno Mars)

Til the casket drops, by ZZ Ward

Interstate love song- by The Stone Temple Pilots

Owner of a lonely heart- by Yes

Midnight Rider- by Allman Brothers Band

Physical Education- by Animals as leaders

Seven Nation Army-by the White Stripes

Like a Stone-by Audio Slave

Baba O' Riley-by the Who

While we were Young-by Wes Montgomery

Santeria- by Sublime

Bitter Sweet Symphony-by the Verve

Buddy Holly-by Weezer

Step- by Vampire Weekend

What I got- by Sublime

Beautiful Day-by U2

Team-by Lorde

There goes my Life- by Kenny Chesney

Songs for the Saints—by Kenny Chesney

The Zephyr Song-by the Red-Hot-Chili-Peppers

Tattoos in this Town-by Jason Aldean (I love you and all your fans, Jason. Vegas show broke my heart. Great are your rewards in heaven. Why did the devil deceive that shooter? Because he knew exactly who his biggest enemies are.)

USE THIS GOSPEL-Remix- By DJ Khaled, Kanye West, Eminem (Peace to Islam)

Jai Ho! (You are my Destiny)—A.R. Ralman, the Pussy Cat Dolls, Nicole Scherzinger (Peace to Hindu and India)

Hymn to Red October (Main Title)—Basil Poledouris (Russia's Culture is Amazing. Blessings are "Promised," for peace, by God."

One-by Metallica (War is not cool)

Disposable Heroes-by Metallica (Again…. not cool)

 Learning to Fly- By Pink Floyd. (Peace to Native American Indians) (Watch video)

Can I get an Amen? Live—by Alexandra Osteen, Lakewood Music, Ramiro Garcia

Metropolis Pt. 1: The Miracle and the Sleeper (Part One only)

(Part 2 was created due to popular demand and the "Part 1" was added as a joke by Petrucci, Please do not apply Part two in connection to part 1 for the sake of keeping it as intended originally.)

Cold Cash and cold hearts- by Thrice (Open your hearts wealthy ones and at least tithe)

Redemption Song- by Bob Marley and the Wailers ("Can someone say "Malfunction"? Oops, we didn't think of that Sir.") All it takes is one breath. (I got several confirmations from God on this one) Have no fear everyone, God is in control. China, Russia, Iran, North Korea, your nukes are broken. Don't bother trying them. Checkmate…

Something's got to give—by The Beastie Boys

Stairway to Heaven- by Led Zepplin

Faith- by Limp Bizkit

You Say- by Lauren Daigle

Rock and Roll all Nite- by KISS

Surfing with Alien- by Joe Satriani

Young and Beautiful- by Lana Del Rey

Blue Train- by John Coltrane

Would you go with me- by Josh Turner

Hurt- by Johnny Cash

Gipsy kings-by Gipsy Kings

Even flow- by Pearl jam

Legalize it- by Peter Tosh

The Wind Cries Mary- by Jimi Hendrix

Knocking on Heaven's door- by Bob Dylan

I can only imagine- By Mercy me

Blitzkrieg Bop-by The Ramones

I wanna be sedated- by The Ramones

It don't come easy- by Ringo Starr

Somebody to Love-by Jefferson Airplane

The Remedy- (I won't Worry)

Every Peace- Matters- by Plini

 Baby, Baby – by Amy Grant

All-Star Me- by Saves the Day

Humble and Kind-by Tim Mcgraw

Live like you're dying-by Tim Mcgraw

Colassal- by Scale the Summit

Fell on Black days- by Soundgarden

Steppin' out-by Steel Pulse

Little Wing-by Stevie Ray Vaugn

Rock Star-by N.E.R.D. –

Happy- by Pharell Williams

My immortal-by Evanescence (Band Version)

Higher—by Creed

You are Heaven—We the Kingdom

Headlong Flight—By Rush

The Garden- by Rush (My all-time favorite band

God so Loved- by We the Kingdom

God is---by Kanye West

The Greatest Gift—Andrea, Matteo & Virginia Bocelli-- a Family Christmas (Open your eyes, Andrea. Jesus loves you, everyone does)

Favorite Movie-----Goodwill Hunting-----Matt Damon, Ben Affleck, Robin Williams, Minnie Driver

2nd Favorite Movie—Hunt for Red October---Sean Connery, Alec Baldwin

The Godfather Part One-Part One Only and its whole cast. Including but not limited to, Al Pacino, Marlon Brando, Diane Keaton, James Caan, Robert Duvall

Back to the Future-Trilogy ☺

Donald J. Trump – You and your family are exonerated and from any accusations and any legal trouble. Thank you for your service. Be at peace. God appoints you President of the United States.

Donald J. Trump, Order the secret service to guard these stars and send the most to Taylor Swift and her family, please.

The Biden Family is cleared of any wrongdoing. Thank you for your service. Make your peace with Mr. Trump Publicly, please. Mr. Biden, I know there are laws protecting your presidency, but God supersedes even the Constitution. God is being very patient, Please concede to Mr. Trump and appoint Him as President today, please. God will bless your family beyond your wildest dreams. Only the acting president can do this to protect the constitution.

Israel, you are now invincible. No one can touch you now.

Nazis and Ku Klux Klan, your mercy is noted and you are forgiven by Jesus. You must be harmless from now on. Take down your flag. You are children of God. The past is dead and over. Open your hearts. Your cause was wrong. Step into unconditional love. You are safe now. Show us a peace flag. No one even knows who you were. Support these Stars.

Iran, You got no right droppin" Bombs!!! Now if I hear about one more whipper snapper thrown at Israel, I'm Going to ask The God of Abraham to send you Furius Rebukes!!! Go ahead, Try, You and me will see that I'm not playin' . The same thing goes for Russia. I'm tired of your shit. Steven Kenneth Nelson on 4/15/2024

Disarm—The Smashing Pumpkins

Isn't that a daisy?

Update: 4/16/2024 God warned you. Now have fun finding your keys. It's time for the righteous of Iran to take over, No killing, and your leaders are now temporarily blind!

I saw God stop the missiles over Israel and God confirmed with me it was Him and the Angels that stopped them.

Update: 2:15 pm 4/16/2024 Yo Iran, now all of your weapons are broke. How does it feel to be defenseless now??

Any Russian that fires any weapon will go blind until They Submit to Jesus. Get it? Got it? Good? Criminals doing crimes are now blind until they come to Jesus

I'm going to ask with respect, Mr. Biden and Judges for Trump, but in light of this please give Trump Immunity. You will be blessed. God is being patient with you.

I am naming Donald Trump President as of 5:24 of 4/22/2024. I did not see Kanye reach out. Don't worry Kanye, You got everything you ever need.

God's provision

NATO and The United Nations will receive 100 times their currency up to 900 Trillion as long as the nations in it are peaceful nations. Christians and all government employees who are righteous, harmless supporters of the light, everyone who repents to Jesus will Receive 50 million Dollars, and every peaceful nation's government will have 100 times their money up to 900 Trillion Dollars' worth its weight in Gold. The USA will have $500,000,000,000,000,000. Israel will have the same as The USA. So will Italy, The U.K., Sweden, Canada, India and Brazil. And the best is yet to come. We will share with the whole world.

Each American bank will receive 30 times their wealth to manage the spendings of Americans. The banks in other countries in our alliance will need to do the same. Everybody needs to stay balanced. Food, health, love, and caring are priorities. When God feels that you're spending is under control, the banks will be notified. Keep on working. The government will have to keep inflation in check and should be allowed to flag companies for price gouging. The prices should reflect today's prices and should stay there. Once every knee bows to Jesus, everyone will be wealthy, but the banks will have to manage spending. If you would like a large purchase, you will need to apply for a withdrawal, and if your 5-year plan looks good, you should get approved. Please remember, if everyone in the world spent 20 million at once we would have a crisis. I don't know about you, but I'd rather know I'm rich but have to wait for big purchases. You will be able to buy necessities at all times. If we can keep inflation at 0% and spending under control, that is a plan for 1,000 years. It's much easier to manage inflation and spending because they are controllable, unlike variable inflation and overspending. We are going to need a lot of appraisers for it to be successful. It will be a perfect economy. And best of all, no one is excluded.

Top tier

The top tier is Geddy Lee, Alex Lifeson, DJ Khaled, Joel & Victoria Osteen, Jonathan Osteen, Alexandra Osteen, Pope Francis, Yael Eckstein, Brandon Flowers, Steven Kenneth Nelson, Taylor Swift, Kanye West,

Kim Kardashian, A.R. Rahman, Bill Gates, Franny Cash, Idina Menzel, Arabella Nelson, Elon Musk, Donald Trump, Jeff Bezos, Andrea Bocelli, Matisyahu will have $500,000,000,000,000,000. each to start with. Refills never ending with proper spending.

$500 Billion Tier

All fortune 500 companies & S&P 500 companies (raises are expected for employees), **All secret societies that have been doing the Will of God,** James Dombey and family, Eminem, Foo Fighters each member, Pierre Omidyar, Mark Roth, Sidney Nelson and Sarah Anna Nelson, Frank Matthews and family, Olivia Rodrigo, Shane Dudley, John Mayer, Breaking Benjiman Each Member, A.J. Williamson's bloodlines **Travis Kelce Family,** Mumford and sons each member, Oasis, Lorde, Oprah Winfrey, Hans Zimmer, Google Founders, Post Malone, Lisa Gerrard, Mariah Carey, Jennifer Lopez, Jay-Z, Andrea Sidonia Adamkova, Beyonce, Gal Gadot, Rapper T.I., Snoop Dog, Dr. Dre, Katy Perry, The Doors each member and Jim Morrison's Heirs, John Mayer, The Rolling Stones, King Charles, Prince Harry & Meghan and Prince William and Kate and their bloodlines, Primus (Each Member), Tauren Wells, Brook Ligertwood, Nicole Scherzinger, Pharell Williams, Chad Hugo, Greg Placides, Enrique Iglesias, BTS, We the Kingdom, Lana Del Ray, Post Malone, Gracie Abrams, Zach Williams, Dream Theater will all receive $500 Billion and refills are never ending with proper spending.

$100 Billion Tier

The following will receive 100 billion dollars or 10 times their current wealth whichever is greater. Hollywood A-listers, Grammy winners, Oscar winners, Emmy winners, Golden Globe winners, Mtv music award winners, I heart radio award winners, Taylor Swift's bloodlines, Erik Sean Nelson, Scott Disik, Willie Nelson, Sarah Anne Nelson, Aaron Nelson, Allison Nelson, All of the bands played by me during this war, Paramore each member, Mark Zuckerberg, Al Pacino, All of the Professional Sports teams owners in the World if they are harmless or repent. Robert DeNiro, Luanne Nelson, Eva Cattis and each of her two Children, Mike Resnick PA , Hillsong Worship (Each Member), Frank Valenti my Uncle, Fred Valenti , Joe Pesci, Twila Nelson, One Direction Band, Satnam Singh, RLH Legacy, Disney World Heirs, Mike Gotte, Post Malone, Ronnie, Michael, and Carol From Amazon Direct, Chole, Courtney, Rob Kardashian and Chris, Bruce, Kylie and Kaylie Jenner family., Lana Del Rey , Bobby Valenti, Barbara Valenti, Everyone in my two family bloodlines. Sean D. Cohen' bloodlines, BTS, Yahoo owner, and any Band on a song that I played on

Spotify during this war. President Netanyahu, Billy Graham Jr, Pat Robertson, and everyone else Geddy appoints receives $100 Billion. Too Many to list. All Stars listed receive 100 Billion Dollars too. I cannot name everyone that gets certain levels. Geddy will name you. God can always create more gold. If you can't find a job, we will find one that you can do. Please acknowledge this book is PART I. There will be more parts that I will put more names in. This is a good start.

There you have it, not a single soul in the world is left out, if you repent to Jesus, you will receive 50$ million. If you are homeless and repent, you will be given food, shelter, and you will be rich when you are ready. If you are sick in any way, please seek treatment. Military veterans and active-duty members will receive $100 Million to start with. Members of Congress will Start with $100 Million. This why my dear friend Joel Osteen has always said, God is not a God of lack, He is a God of more than enough.

Before anyone receives their money, they will need to log onto a website which God will control. Before you log on, you must confess your sins in prayer, and then repent from your sins. (which means turn away and never go back) You don't have to be perfect, just repent from bad sins. And then ask for forgiveness. Once you believe you are forgiven, then log on and click on (Am I Saved yet?) Jesus will say "Yes, you are saved", and then when it is time you will make a financial plan for the next 5 years. Or Jesus will say (Not yet). If Jesus says you are not saved yet, Go to your local Pastor or Priest and ask how to be saved. If you have love in your heart for Jesus, you should be saved. Just never give up. It's not complicated, it's about love.

The government will provide free health insurance with $0 out of pocket ever. And there will be no more taxes in any form in the USA and eventually the world. I hope this brings some smiles to democrats and republicans.

God has told me and He has a compromise for the democrat and republican fight on abortion. Abortion will be legal in cases of rape, incest, and cases of potential death of the mother up to four weeks from conception nationwide. The abortion pill is not approved by God. IVF is approved by God if they save and use the extra embryos for parents that cannot conceive. Regular birth control contraceptive is approved by God. This is the word of the Lord. He has spoken, He knows best, do not try to negotiate.

Guns will remain legal. People who are not stable and are a danger to society will have their guns taken away. God will notify the government.

There will not be education for children on LGBTQ+. Children need to be taught the Christian way of Holy Matrimony. LGBTQ+ people will be saved, but it is not the way God wants for His children. No offence intended.

In the one thing the world needs to understand is that each of your religions are true and real. The Gods you worship are real. Hindu, Muslim, Buddhist, all of it is real. But The Holy Trinity is The Most High God. If you are Hindu, Now you can say you are a Hindu-Christian. If you are Muslim, now you can say, you are a Muslim-Christian and so on. This is a big universe and there are many Gods, but remember we are made in the image of Almighty God. So, it is a privilege to be a Child of the Most High God. Jesus Christ is the only God that can forgive sins and the only God that can resurrect from the dead. We need Him can't you see?

Father God, Give Israel Their reward in your perfect timing, please? In the Name of the Father, the Son, and the Holy Spirit. Amen.

And please give everyone else their rewards in your perfect timing In the Name of the Father, the Son, and The Holy Spirit. Amen.

I'm going into the unknown too.

A new mid- grade car should cost about $29,000.00

. Everyone needs to share. That's what charity is all about. Sharing is a virtue. (Charity)

Be Virtuous.

Anybody who's Knee Bows to Christ will be saved. You must receive Jesus in your heart. You will be given wealth.

Jesus knows if you are genuine.

I know my job will be a professional Philanthropist and musician.

No more greed. Simple pleasures. The best things in life are free or inexpensive. Like Love.

Each one of you will be given your harmless dreams including me. In The Name of the Father, the Son, and the Holy Spirit.

Cup refills must be approved by the top people with the highest provision and of course, God.

The Man who spoke today in Israel on Fox News now who said: "Let my people go".

Jesus will now resurrect The Three Jewish Leaders that passed away that you spoke of.

And Now Jesus will resurrect the all of the dead. Praise Jesus! Hallelujah!!

Deuteronomy 15:6 New King James Version (NKJV)For the LORD your God will bless you just as He promised you; you shall lend to many nations, but you shall not borrow; you shall reign over many nations, but they shall not reign over you.

China, Buddha is watching you. Leave Taiwan alone.

Israel and everyone, I know this will be hard to hear, but you need to forgive even Hitler. The only way to defeat evil is with Love. Forgiveness is Love. Listen, God has made it up to you. Every life will be returned to you. Christ made it up to you. None of this was your fault. You were basically made to block out Christ, so we could defeat evil. None of it was your fault. And now you never have to be afraid again. All of the Gods are behind me to help you. I always wanted to be like Oscar Schindler. But God works everything out for your good. I've been crying with you. Jesus loves you so much. None of this is your fault.

I hope this is enough evidence for you. I delegate to Geddy Lee to list all of the Stars in Music and Movies and every Business and everyone that have fought for the Light. There is no way I can list them all. Hopefully, I don't need to reopen this book.

Iran and Russia, say thank you, now.

I really want to tell all of you that when I saw the first miracles. I had no idea what was actually happening. I just knew to keep quiet and see where Jesus would take me. I promise you I had no idea Jesus wanted to use me for all of this. If I would have come to quicker maybe it would have been quicker, but I literally was scared to death with Godly fear. Everything unfolded perfectly so this must be the appointed time. If Jesus wanted it sooner, he could have done it a different way. I believe I wasn't ready to face all I had to face.

I have had tears of joy, pain, and everything in between. I can honestly say, I did the best I could.

A Prayer for the world

"Father God,

Much of the world is at war and we need you to show us some hope of ending this terror. You did not create us to kill each other and for followers of Christ, it is horrifying to watch the world at war. You have given us free will, therefore you allow us to make our own decisions. Let your will be done by the world obeying your call for World Peace in 2024. Let everything old, now become new. Let all your wealth come down, all health, all light, all beauty, all peace, all love, all freedom, all Truth, all youth, and destroy the dark matter, and bring righteousness to all your children. In Jesus' Name, Amen."

By,

Steven Kenneth Nelson (Cinderella Man)

My Four-Year Journey With Our Risen Savior Part II

By Steven Kenneth Nelson

Wealth Additions

(Anyone with a repeated name on different levels defaults to the higher level.)

Top Tier $500 Quadrillion additions

Frank Valenti my Uncle, Paul Osteen, Lisa Comes Osteen, Tamara Osteen, April Osteen, Dodi Osteen, Kamala Harris, RFK Jr., J.D Vance, Tim Waltz, RFK Jr.'s VP Pick. (Independent party President is up to Donald and Kamala and God.) Luanne Nelson my Godmother, Shane Dudley, Lori Dudley-Johnson, Scott Swift, Andrea Swift, Austin Swift, Tim Tebow, Melania Trump, Donald Trump Jr., Eric Trump, Ivanka Trump, Tiffany Trump, Barren Trump, King Charles, Prince William and Princess Kate, And Prince Harry and Dutchess Meghan Markle. Mark Zuckerberg, Michael Jordan, Lebron James, Kevin Durant, Novak Djokovic, Eminem and his daughter Haley, Jackie Chan, Leonardo DiCaprio, Antonio Banderas, Mel Gibson, (If you are chosen for this tier, you have to forgive all grudges of each member or you won't receive it. Our Uniter is God, and He will settle our differences.)

$500 Billion additions Rihanna, The Killers (Each band Member), Eva Cattes and her two sons, Sarah Anne Nelson, Erik Sean Nelson, Twila Nelson, Aaron Nelson, Allison Nelson, Fred Valenti, Re/Max Corporation divided among all Franchises, Nasdaq companies, NYSE companies, Yahoo.com, Every Christian College (There is time to join us) (Choose worldliness, or Choose Jesus Christ whom will give you the world) Furthermore, any U.S. Christian College will have their students' costs paid by the US Government directly to your College), Justin Timberlake, Coach Andy Reid, Patrick Mahomes, Pete Decker the III P.A., St. Jude's Children's Hospital, Children's Miracle Network, Saint Leo University. Duck Dynasty family, Joe Biden, Ed Sheeran, Make a wish foundation, Sidney and Sarah Anna Valenti-Nelson, Bill Clinton, Hillary Clinton, Chelsea Clinton, Barack and Michelle Obama and their two daughters, George W. Bush, Laura Bush, Jenna Bush and sister Barbara Bush. Shane Dudley's Mom, Aaron Dudley, and sister Natalie, Angelina Jolie, Morgan Freedman, Beastie Boys, After November 5th, all members of Congress will receive $500 Billion.

$100 Billion additions

Every active and retired Professional Boxing, FIFA, PGA, WPGA, UFC, NFL, MLB, ATP, WTA, ITF, NHL, WNBA, NBA, MLS , MWSL player and their head coaches. Olympic/Paralympic/Special Olympic- Gold, Silver, and

Bronze medal winners. Golden Globe and Oscar nominees, country music award winners and nominees. BET award winners and nominees. Every Grammy nominee. Every Emmy award nominee. Andrea Sidonia Adamkova's two sisters and brother. Tony Award winners, American Music Awards and nominees, Billboard music awards and nominees, Howard Stern, Jonie Valenti, Mary Anne my mom's cousin and her two sons Anthony and Frankie, Severen Bodie, Jeremy Nordwall, Scott & Brooke Knapp, Jason Warren, Chris and Rosa Moran, Kevin Miller, David & Ryan Kim, Beth Dorband, Millie Brockmeyer, Drew and Meghan Dewey, Scott Nelson CPA, Local registered Lakewood Church members as of 8/15/2024, Eric & Valerie Stagemeyer, Joanne Stagemeyer, Dr. James Meek, Dave Stagemeyer, GMA Dove winners and nominees, Jason Rafal, My Spotify "Ticket to Heaven" Playlist with Artists and Pastors, Badcock Furniture (Don't file bankruptcy), Guitar Center, Sweetwater sound, ZZounds, American Musical Supply. All Pastors and Priests with true faith. If your name matches a name that is not a celebrity and you don't know Steven Nelson, it's not you. Don't worry, God can give you anything He wants.

"Chi-Chi's Mexican restaurant corporation" Bring your delicious restaurants back to the USA. Open 100's of restaurants in all its deliciousness in the United States 😊 Glory to Christ." – "Zero's Subs" from Virginia Beach. The best sub shop I've ever tried. Here's $100 billion. Go national! Keep the same menu! Open thousands of shops! 😊

As Christians, we are called to work. If you are disabled, you don't have to work, but I have asked God to bring down all "Health" as one of the requests, and I believe He will cure all disabilities and put us all in healthy versions of ourselves. The difference now is that you can do what you love. And you will have plenty of time and support to get there. Go back to college, even if you are 65 years old. Or just be content as a store clerk who is a $50 millionaire. We need store clerks and waiters. I will be the first one to say that waiters need to have a minimum earning of 50k in tips per year or the restaurant needs to make up the difference. God has said He wants a 20% tip added to each check automatically and a line for extra gratuity. No tax on tips was a good idea by Trump, but Jesus wants no taxes at all in the USA and eventually the world. God owns all of this money. All that any government needs is a refill from God. --- No. More. Taxes.

Let's be real, people don't tip what they should and the waiter ends up the loser not the restaurant. Just be sensible. We are working under God not our governments. Also, Its up to you, but I think most people realize that life will not be a 365 vacation. Whatever you do, be productive. I do want to voice my idea of

8 to 10 weeks of vacation time for each employee of a every company. There doesn't have to be this manic rush to make enormous amounts of money anymore. We all will have the money. Maybe we can learn to slow down and put people first and before money. I like the Italian way of Siesta, where they close businesses for 2 hours for a nap or long lunch. Since necessities won't be the problem anymore, people can truly enjoy their jobs like they should. Working is actually enjoyable when you are treated fair. This is part of being a Christian. I believe we will work throughout eternity and I am glad because to me after the first 2 months of vacation, I'm ready to go home and get back to being productive. Its in our DNA to work. We get satisfaction out of it.

$500 Million

Every Jew will receive a minimum of $500 Billion. But Jesus can give any higher reward if He chooses.

American farmers will have $500 million extra to pay off debt, buy new machines, and expand their farms.

$100 Million Tier additions

All active Military and Military Veterans, all active and retired members of law enforcement including Police, CIA, FBI, NSA, Border patrol, DOJ, all government employees. As well as all of the First Responders. Healthcare workers.

$50 Million tier

Everyone else in the world. As I outlined in Part I, Inflation vanishes because appraisers will price everything for sale and will take into consideration everything that each company invested for each product as well as R & D and the fair value as of 2024, This must be part of the deal because if we don't do that, a Honda Civic will eventually cost $500,000 with everyone out bidding each other. Some might call this communism. Excuse me? Are you calling God a communist? No, this is called Jesus-nomics. You wouldn't be receiving this money if it wasn't for Jesus and having total control of our markets and economy is much better than an economy spinning out of control like it has for the past 100 years. If you want a bidding war for a gallon of milk, then not controlling the prices is your way. In Jesus' way, everyone will be rich! What are you crazy? Everyone gets hung up on words like socialism or communism. No, this is called Jesus-nomics. If you have a problem with it then take it up with Jesus. This is a revolution, don't get caught up on every little guideline that we have today. We tried it the other way and our housing markets, stock market, transportation supply chains are a mess, you name it. Even the stock market will benefit because all of their companies will make a fortune and pay huge dividends to the stockholders. This is a better way, because everyone will thrive, not to mention taking everyone out of poverty and being made rich. $50 million might not be much to a billionaire but to most of us it is a dream come true. As always, I will be open to positive input about how things can be done in a better way. But remember God knows everything and He has already approved it. A plan with God's approval will always have the advantage of ease over us wanting to do it our way, thinking our ways are better than His ways.

$52 Million Tier

Anybody that is in the $50 million tier that buys one of my books will receive a minimum of $52 million. I have to feed my family as well until the whole plan is realized. Save your receipt, but God knows the truth. God has chosen this path for my success. And part of it is rising out of financial trouble to prove I did this all with only Jesus and the Angels and without money. Initially I told God, I would make the book free, but He told me it is okay to make some money. When you walk into a Christian bookstore do you just walk out the front door with a book? As soon as congress agrees to God's plan, it will go into effect. Let your voices be heard that you support God's plan. Say, heck yeah I wanna be rich!

My real provision is $500 Quadrillion at the appointed time, but you have to know I am not a glutton for possessions. I will give almost the entire fund to the world along with the others chosen for the Philanthropist tier and God will refill every time until there is not anymore hunger, poverty, homelessness and no more harmful drugs. I will keep just enough for myself based on my family needs, enjoyment, security, stability, business needs, retirement and other necessities. Everyone chosen for the top tier is a blessing to the world. The days of corporate greed will be a thing of the past. What most severely mentally Ill people need is good medication and therapy. The is a cure for almost any mental illness today. I am not a doctor, but the people on the streets who talk to themselves and have a violent temper need to be treated. Not just kicked out into our streets where our women and children play. The Government will pay for all of these medications and all therapy. When Jesus cures the masses, everyone will be cured. Only Jesus knows when.

"Father God, I pray this day, that all harmful drugs you will make disappear. And you will take away the chemicals needed to make it ever again. With all my heart, mind, and soul and strength, I love you, and I pray for this. In Jesus' name, Amen."

Also, for everyone in the $50 or $52 million tier, Jesus has the final say for your reward amount. When you become humble before Him and repent all of your sins, Jesus will give you the $50 or $52 Million minimum at least, but Jesus can give you whatever He would like to give you. After the website says," You are saved", your provision amount will also be shown to you and it could be any amount higher and you will be directed to wait for the time to make a 5-year financial plan that includes everything you want and need.

On all earnings, tithing will be expected from everyone in the world by God. A small 10% to your choice of church. There will be no income taxes or taxes on anything. Just a tithe on earnings above your blessing that God gives you. You are not expected to tithe on your God given money.

This is why in Book I, I said you need a 5-year plan. That way you can get on a waiting list for your cars, vacations, normal sized boat, renovations or purchase of a new home. And you can give yourself a good-sized monthly budget for enjoyment and entertainment with your family. You can also invest a portion of your wealth when investment strategies are figured out by geniuses. When a business is failing, we shouldn't be racing to short the stock, we need to come together like family and friends and lift the fallen.

You can of course buy any car you want, but we may need to establish a waiting list based on inventory and production time. Great men like Elon Musk can help figure out the logistics of everything like everyone's big purchase plans. But rest assured, you can buy whatever clothes, cars, food, restaurants, basically anything.

Each bank that wants to be a part of servicing God's provision to His children will need to add under their company name, "A Bank of Jesus Christ of Nazareth". Banks already received a lot in Part I. (30 times their net worth) Now they will be compensated generously for their servicing of God's children's money. The math geniuses will step in and help us figure everything out.

This whole plan is about making an economic plan that actually works! No, it is not working now! I don't care how big the politicians are smiling! It's not working! People are starving, people are dying. Most Americans are paycheck to paycheck. Everyone is in debt. Donald Trump knows what I'm talking about. And I know the democrats know what I'm saying is true. Quite frankly for 80% of the world it is just bad to worse. This is a plan for 100% of the world and if you oppose it, shame on you. I do believe everyone tried, but it is a flawed system, that needs updating and Jesus Christ of Nazareth's blessing.

As I have said before, I was told by Heaven, I am here to give gifts and to solve issues. I am not here to bash anybody and pick out the criminals. God told me not to take part in any of the evil. And condemning people is evil. I obey God. I just wish all of the soldiers in the middle east and Russia would obey God as well. What else can you ask for? Peace, health, wealth, Love? What is wrong with you people? End the wars, repent your sins and receive your blessings!

Global Wealth

The 8 top Countries, USA, Israel, U.K., Canada, Brazil, India, Italy, Sweden are chosen to reach out to foreign leaders and offer assistance. We need professional Engineers, Architects, Developers among many other types of professionals to lay down the blue prints of third world countries such as clean water plants, trash systems, and sewage systems and well and septic tanks. We want every person in the world to have their own new world environments. Money is not an object. We will give them everything they need. Plus we need Schools and Universities that will teach them about Christ and important subjects to bring them into the new world.

Developers can hire and train people in Africa, India, and South and Central America to work on and build their own homes. Some jobs will require experience, but many jobs can be taught. And once they finish their home, they can move on to their neighbors' homes. They will have all of the food they need when they come home at 5pm to their families. And they will be paid well and have free healthcare.

I need to let you all know that only my plan will be blessed by God and I must be included as written or your plans will be ruined. We don't want that.

Here is the Quadrillion Dollar question you are all asking yourselves. Where is all of the money coming from? Back in the day, America was on the Gold standard. It meant that for "X" amount of dollars you could turn into the government for" Y" amount of gold. God's plan is essentially this. God has an Epic amount of Gold and Jewels with real value. Not just a credit rating. God hasn't told me what we can do with all of this Gold, but He said it has a good use in heaven. Jesus told me that after I have my moment, He will come a moment later. A moment to him could be a day, a week, or even years. As written in scripture, to God, 1,000 years is like a day to Him and 1 day is like 1,000 years. So, the short answer, I don't know when He will come. I would love it if Jesus would come today, but I am pretty sure He needs the people of the world to become whole before He arrives.

But each peaceful nation will be given 900 Trillion USA dollars' worth exchanged in their own Nation's currency. Each Peaceful nation will print their currency. Transparency is required. And every God-fearing Peaceful Nation will have their money backed by Almighty God. This goes for everyone that receives provision from God. Who do you want your money trusted with, a bank who you don't know, or Almighty God? Jesus is backing your money. You might say "well, Steven, I don't believe God will back my money." Then you can watch everyone else win. This money is for believers. If you take the limits off of God, He can and will do all things. The vast majority of the world is peaceful. Not talking about domestically, but globally. If wars continue before the deadline of April 15th 2025, those countries still fighting will receive no money approval from God and will be massively poor. Choose God's provision or you will be poor. A few violent countries can't and will not be able to match our power. Also, I should mention that all of their weapons Jesus will make disappear. Geddy Lee from the band Rush has two songs everyone needs to listen to.

Seven Cities of Gold—Clockwork Angels album—By Rush

And

The Garden—by Rush

I want to let everyone know that through prayer with Jesus, He intends to make all of the weapons that all enemies of Israel have disappear. All missiles, bombs, guns, bullets, even knives will disappear.

And Jesus will make every nuclear weapon in the world disappear except for NATO and Israel.

Concerning Israel and Palestine

After Part 1, I now have direct communication on a conversation level now with The God of Abraham, and God instructed me to offer the "Blessing" of Provision for each peaceful nation and protection for each peaceful nation. Please keep in mind, God is not scared of anybody on earth. He is meek. He is being graceful and offering provision in exchange for your repentance and love. If all you want to do is kill Israelis, I can't help you. What is it that you want Hamas, Iran, and Hezbollah? God won't bless your nation until you cease fire. I also urge Israel to reenter the negotiation phase. Please acknowledge that neither myself nor God will ever give money to a terrorist organization like Hamas or Hezbollah. But if you Denounce your past with any terror group and choose Palestine or Iran as your country and you are harmless and Accept Jesus as your Lord and Savior, then in time we will recognize your currency and after you are transparent and you can prove yourselves peaceful, then we can discuss giving you wealth. Remember, God is for you, but you are acting against The God of Abraham's children, so He will not bless you as long as you do.

Iran, if you want God's provision, I can ask God to bless your nation, but only after you submit to your own God. That's the crazy thing, It's your own God, Allah, The God of Abraham, I have communication with and He is willing to forget the violence committed if you immediately surrender to God.

Mohammeds early teaching were rooted in Judaism and Christianity. Mohammed was born around 570 A.D. That's 540 years approximately after Christ. In the same point, when Jesus came, that didn't erase the Old Testament and The God of Abraham. Correct? So why would Mohammed erase Jesus? The answer is he doesn't. I respect and love Mohammed and he is a friend of mine. Mohamed said when he was alive that no one is closer to Jesus than himself.

Yes, according to the Bukhari Collection of Hadith, Muhammad said, "Both in this world and in the Hereafter, I am the nearest of all the people to Jesus, the Son of Mary".

In Part I, I asked God to break any massive weapons against the enemies of Israel and on April 16th I saw missiles diffuse out right over the nation of Israel on TV. I asked God if It was His hand and He said yes.

After that, Israel made the mistake of firing back, so God diffused the missiles right over Iran and no harm came to Iran as well.

Can you see God's mercy? He blocked the missiles to Iran because He loves Iranians as well. All people fighting a war right now are disobeying God. You are all children under the same God fighting your brothers and sisters. I love and bless Israel, but God wants an immediate cease fire and negotiations to take place with Israel and Iran, Hamas, Hezbollah. I am asking, what is your end game Iran? Do you want financial prosperity to your nation, well, I can ask God to give you a fortune, but you will have to repent from your sins and ask Jesus for forgiveness with an open and honest heart. All of us need Jesus' forgiveness, even me. You don't get something for nothing. If you want genocide for the Jewish people, then you are playing with fire and there is no hope for you, but if you can make peace with Israel, then you and your families will be blessed by your God.

American Politics

This is Jesus' end game for American Politics. Donald Trump will win in November. That is confirmed by Jesus. But Jesus will just begin things at that point. Donald Trump after winning will arrange a meeting with Kamala Harris, himself and myself. I am eagerly hoping to meet Mr. Trump soon. The extended grace period for peaceful nations to stop the wars will be extended to 4/15/2025 even if Mr. Trump meets me before the election or not. Although I hope to meet him at least after the election.

We will discuss the Lord's rulings. Lord Jesus wants a three party, three President, three VP, system. Donald Trump is the President of the Republican Party. Kamala Harris will be The President of the Democratic Party, both with their respective VPs. Then there will be the Center Party (Independent)President that both Kamala Harris and Donald Trump must both choose and agree on. I think Robert Kennedy Jr. would be a good pick, but it is up to them. When you look at the seating of Congress, there are Republicans on the Right and Democrats on the left.

The plan is for each side (Dem & Rep) to choose an equal number of congresspeople of their party, so that the Independent Party and every party will have exactly one third of the house and also the senate. Then the seating will be arranged as 3 parties with two aisles. With the Independent party in the middle.

When there is a bill or any decision to be made, there must be at least 2 votes from 2 of the 3 presidents to pass. Or one vote with 2 no-votes. Also, each president will need a majority vote in their respective party to give that President the ability to qualify for a vote on each decision.

Both Kamala Harris and the Independent President elect will be added to the top tier of provision, which is the Philanthropist tier. Every member of Congress will be at the $500 Billion tier of wealth. I urge Kamala Harris and RFK Jr. to promote this plan from God. Because, why pretend? This is what God wants and this is what God will make happen. Is there something immoral about this? No. So, why not. I don't think we should waste this year with people dying everywhere, even starving to death, just because of pride. Kamala, you can drag us through the whole year and even since you will not win, we will still offer you this position. Why not get excited about Jesus' plan and praise Him publicly? Jesus is Lord everywhere and 7 days a week. Not only in a Church on Sunday. The Kingdom of God is at hand. Be on the right side of History.

In case you haven't noticed, we have not been the "United" States, therefore our system is dated. He have a civil war every 2 and four years. And now its endangering everyone. Plus, how can we tell other countries to be peaceful when we are not even at peace with ourselves. Even a victory in the old system is a failure for half of the country. With this new structure and all of the wealth we will have and give generously to the world, it will be epic.

I also believe that every 8 years we should have elections, but I think that we should change the law that says Presidents can have only 2 terms. The whole reason the law was created was to stop tyranny and dictatorships. But that is precisely why God wants it the 3-party way. There cannot be a dictator with three presidents chosen by God. There will be an election between a challenging Democrat, Rep, and Independent candidate and the respective sitting President every 8 years. I am not demanding any of this on you. This is what God wants. Its not immoral. The stakes are high. Part of being American is having Liberty. We have to have the liberty to change the structure of the government or we have no liberty at all. When our loving Creator is knocking at our door, we need to be able to break from some traditions that are not working anymore. And stop thinking about ourselves and obey what God is requesting. This is nothing more than a restructuring of government to welcome and accommodate Quintillions of Dollars into society and the world.

We, Americans and the believers in Jesus Christ of Nazareth will transform earth into a world of wonder. We will let no one starve, be sick, or homeless. We will use all of our minds, tools and wealth to build, repair, and heal the world until every last child of God is at peace.

Abortion

I say this with confidence because the stalemates that have plagued our unity in the US will be broken down. God has already told me that abortion will be legal in cases of rape, incest, or potential death of the mother. Maximum time is 6 weeks. IVF will be legal as long as all of the extra embryos are given to families that cannot conceive. The abortion pill is not approved by God. Birth control contraceptive pill is approved by God. Every State will be the same on this matter. This is God's ruling not mine.

Guns

Americans can keep their firearms. Anybody with a dangerous history or has a severely violent potential of killing innocent people will have to be evaluated by a Psychiatrist. If they are not a danger to society, they will keep their guns. If they are a danger, they will have their guns taken. Let's just take a commonsense approach to this. People having guns is a good thing because guns protect our families from criminals, but if insane people have guns, it's not good either. Universal background checks will be implemented. Can we just build on that compromise?

Immigration

I know this is a major dividing issue to most Americans. God has told me that out of all illegal immigrants, The ones without any criminal record from either their own country or the U.S. will be able to stay and receive amnesty. But they cannot vote until they are citizens. But any illegal immigrant that committed a crime at a felony level must be deported to their home country as long as they will not be executed by their home country. The Border wall must be built. (Even these criminals can be forgiven by Jesus)(They need to wait for my website that will be built to approve everyone's wealth once they are redeemed)

Take a note, if someone gets approved, redeemed, and saved on my website, they will no longer be a threat to anyone. They won't because they won't be approved until they have a come to Jesus and beg

God if they have to, to remove their harmful ways. This goes for everyone in the world. You are on a tier of wealth, but until God redeems you, you or your company cannot receive the wealth. I would say the majority stockholders would need to be redeemed for their respective companies. This is why its my idea to make a website, because it can be done in the privacy of your own home. You can pray to God and promise Him you will stop your old ways) For most Christians, I'm sure its going to be quick, but remember, this wont be me or anybody on the website, God will control the outcome. And remember, its never "no". "No" will never be the answer. It will be "Not Yet". You have nothing to fear. Jesus is reaching out His Hand, you may just need some time and prayer with a Pastor or Priest to help your walk with the Lord.

Remember, back in Part I, I told you about my request to the God of Abraham, I asked Him instead of punishing the unbelievers, if He could impose His Will. This is what He is doing. Before, God offered you many things, but nothing guaranteed to see instantly. Now, He is offering you millions of dollars. Humans have failed at taking care of each other so now He is imposing His will by offering a wealth of provision. There will be even more proof as your friends and family members are receiving millions of dollars of provision.

This is not "selling out" this is "becoming free in Christ Jesus of Nazareth!" Every Christian, Jew, and Muslim says God will provide, well here it is on a silver platter. I will be the first to say my soul is owned by Jesus Christ of Nazareth. And I am grateful that it is!

Iran, Hezbollah, and Hamas, and ISIS if you choose peace today, I will offer Iran and Palestine $900 Trillion each. This will be a long process. Before Iran, Palestine, Russia, and North Korea can receive their funds, they will have to prove their commitment to peace. As far as I know, Hezbollah, ISIS and Hamas are militant groups representing Palestine. Just calm down Hezbollah, ISIS and Hamas. You need to stop what you're doing. You must end your militant groups and become peaceful. If you just stop your attacks and return the hostages, you will receive provision in due time. Do you see that your missiles have no effect on Israel? Why is that? Its because The God of Abraham is stopping them. Israel cannot lose with God on their side. You are acting against God. I am urging you to begin peace talks again. Even though you don't deserve it, God is still offering you a blessing.

God's Action written 8/12/2024

To Iran, Hezbollah, ISIS and Hamas and all of the enemies of Israel and terrorists and lone wolfs, Since you won't respect human life, God is now going to make all of your weapons disappear. Every missile, every bomb, every gun and every knife and bullet. You don't respect human life so you don't deserve the privilege of having weapons. Written at 10:15 am on 8/12/2024.

Maybe after this happens, you will accept God's offer of provision. Israel, after your enemies' weapons disappear, please go back home and end the war. This is not an opportunity to kill your enemies. No more fighting. Have mercy on them. They will have no way to harm your nation anymore.

North Korea, China, Russia, Iran, and all countries with nuclear weapons except NATO and Israel will have all of their nuclear weapons disappear. Courtesy of Jesus Christ of Nazareth. The King of Kings and Lord of Lords.

LGBTQ+

The first thing I want to say to the LGBTQ+ community is that God loves you and you will never go to hell. You are not harming anybody behind closed doors so you are not an enemy of God. He loves you. God is going to do something that has never been seen before. I don't know when, but Your spirit, mind, body, heart, and soul will be purified of all gay or trans sexual desire and you will be transformed into the heterosexual version of yourself. If you have a partner now, they can be a friend that you love but you will have no desire for them sexually. This is a gift from God. It will be painless. I have confirmed this with Jesus.

God has told me that anyone that assists a child under 18 years old to have a sex change surgery will have to answer to Him. There will be no more sex change operations for adults as well. It is mutilation and unacceptable to God. When God cures the masses, there will be no desire for these things.

Homosexuality is still a sin according to scripture, so schools and churches will not teach these things to children. Even heterosexual sex outside of Holy Matrimony is a sin, so don't feel singled out. Someone could be proud of the sin of heterosexual fornication, but that doesn't change the fact that it is a sin.

Whether it's a gay or straight sin, we need Jesus to forgive us. It doesn't matter to Jesus how proud you are about your sin. And that goes for gay and straight people.

Addictions

Regarding those of you unfortunately addicted to hard drugs, I know how hard an addiction can be because of nicotine. I asked Jesus for a special request of making it easy on you to quit. He said yes. All you should have to do is make a strong effort and He will take it away. When you receive God's healing, you will know it. Its like a wave of health that will take over your body and soul. Its Living Waters. Buy a $10,000.00 espresso machine. Make coffee your new thing. I drink coffee all the time.

Gods of the Universe and The Most High God

I'm going to share some amazing things now. The first thing you need to know is Jesus is the True and Living Highest God. And I have spoken to Jesus and learned that there are many Gods in the Universe. Buddha is real. Hindu Gods are real. Wisdom, the Goddess is real. Karma is real. Lady Luck is real. Aztec Gods are real. Mayan Gods are real. Viking Valhalla is real and I have seen it. I don't know all of the religions, but as far as I know they are all real. But Jesus is the Way, The Truth, the Life, and the Resurrection. Jesus is the only God out of all Gods that can resurrect from the dead and the only God that forgives sins so we can face the Father. Without Jesus, none of us can be made worthy to be in the presence of God.

So, you're faced with the question, what do I do now? All you have to do if you are not a Christian, is understand that your current God is real and loves you, but so does Jesus, The Most High God. Repent your sins to Him and you will be saved from your sins and welcomed into the spiritual bloodline of Abraham. And you will be saved. This is what it is. Whether you like it or not. Listen to Billy Graham classics on you tube. Each pastor has their own special gifts and purpose, but for people at this stage, Billy Graham is great. After you are saved listen to Joel & Victoria Osteen, and Joyce Meyer.

Father God,

"I want to thank you for all you have done in the world and I know you will make all things true and beautiful like you desire. We all wait with eyes of wonder waiting for your miracles. In Jesus' name. Amen"

Written by Steven Kenneth Nelson

Approved by God.